OF SUCH IS THE KINGDOM OF HEAVEN

OF SUCH IS THE KINGDOM OF HEAVEN

Teaching the Gospel to Middle-Grade Children
Using Mime, Art, Drama, Gesture, Discussion and Prayer

Sr. Jane Dubrouillet, R.S.C.J.

PAULIST PRESS
New York/Ramsey, N.J./Toronto

Library of Congress
Catalog Card Number: 77-14795

ISBN: 0-8091-2078-X

Published by Paulist Press
Editorial Office: 1865 Broadway, N.Y., N.Y. 10023
Business Office: 545 Island Road, Ramsey, N.J. 07446

Printed and bound in the
United States of America

TABLE OF CONTENTS

page

Introduction 1
Story Gestures 7
Unit 1–The Birth of John the Baptist is Foretold 13
Unit 2–The Birth of Jesus Is Announced............................19
Unit 3–Mary Visits Elizabeth 23
Unit 4–The Birth of John the Baptist.................................27
Unit 5–The Birth of Jesus 33
Unit 6–Jesus Is Presented In The Temple 37
Unit 7–The Wise Men...43
Unit 8–The Flight Into Egypt 49
Unit 9–The Boy Jesus In The Temple 55
Unit 10–The Baptism of Jesus 61
Unit 11–The Call 67
Unit 12–The Marriage Feast At Cana................................73
Unit 13–Jesus Heals A Paralyzed Man..............................79
Unit 14–Jesus Calms A Storm..85
Unit 15–Jairus' Daughter 89
Unit 16–Feeding The Five Thousand 95
Unit 17–Mary And Martha..101
Unit 18–The Ten Lepers..105
Unit 19–Jesus And The Children 109
Unit 20–Zacchaeus 113

WHY TEACH SCRIPTURE TO 8-11 YEAR OLDS?

Young children are eager explorers of truth. Daily they discover the exciting world outside of themselves and want to be a part of it. They probe both reality and myth, unconsciously abstracting concepts and ideals which they incorporate into their lives. These are the years of attitude formation when children are most sensitive, perceptive and alive to impressions. This is the age when they are neither inhibited nor embarrassed to be themselves, and allow others that same freedom.

If this is the age when positive habits and attitudes are easily developed and retained, then this is the moment for the presentation of Scripture.

The Gospel teachings are as simple as the children are themselves. Therefore the method of teaching Scripture must be simple and basic to human nature. The senses have always been the best learning tools. Children who are allowed to move into the life of Jesus with gesture, drama, art and reflection absorb his life. As interaction and sharing evolve, values are internalized and a life experience begins. Children create their attitudes with the Creator. How they see the Gospel will be their secret, and will not necessarily surface in profound statements. But the truth of the message will ease into the fiber of their lives and be a continual reward. Happily, religion teachers can recall the fact that the Gospel is alive with its own teaching, and their job is simply the privilege of watching God at work in these young hearts.

UNIT STRUCTURE

Every Unit has four Sections: *A. TELLING THE STORY, B. ART FORM, C. THE PLAY*, and *D. REFLECTION.*
Below, each Section will be described by the *General Theory, Procedure*, and *Alternatives*. Since flexibility means success in any class situation, the alternatives should be considered an important dynamic.

Section A—TELLING THE STORY

1) GENERAL THEORY
Every child comes alive when a leader says, "Do what I do!" This structure is based on the theory that children are "born mimics" and enjoy a certain security in repetition. This simple way of telling a story, line by line, with gestures, is an enjoyable technique for both student and teacher.

2) PROCEDURE:
Initial Preparation:
—Gestures; Explain the process of repetition with gestures. Act out several gestures and let them guess the symbolism. (See Gesture Key, p. 8).
—Geographical locations; Since gestures are used it is helpful to establish locations and directions in the classroom. Example: Jerusalem to the right of teacher, Galilee to the left, etc. (See Key for Geographical Locations, p. 7.)

Immediate Preparation:
—Explain difficult words and concepts.
Some stories need a brief overview before "the telling." It helps to give a vivid word picture of the setting, the people, and the plot. Showing a picture of the scene is helpful.
—Music:
While telling the story play quiet, slow instrumental music (record player or tape). This can set the mood and will create association when played during other procedures.

Telling the Story:

—Ask the children to stand and repeat after you. Say each line. At the word printed in bold type use the gesture indicated by the number at the end of the line. For this part, assume a solemn attitude, use a story-telling voice, enunciate clearly and then give time for the repetition and gesture. Motivate the children to speak and act as if they were telling the story to an audience for the first time. (Remember, you are their audience—show interest in their repetition.) Some children may not enjoy this type of activity. Let them remain seated and listen.

3) ALTERNATIVES:

It is important to sense the mood of the class. Here are some substitutions for the "repetition-gesture" approach.

—A simple telling of the story.
  This can be done with or without gestures. You might like to map or chalk a scene on the board, or hold up a picture.

—Ask questions which will draw out the story from them.

—Let a few who know the story mime the actions while the others guess the plot.

—Use gestures other than those suggested.

—The whole world of interpretive dance is open to you.

Section B—ART FORM

1) GENERAL THEORY:

Art appeals to all children. This creative form helps them to "get in touch" with the Gospel scene they have heard. They want to transfer their mental image of the story into an expression that is part of their own reality. This reproduction is the second step toward fostering personal contact and identity with Jesus.

PROCEDURE:

Set the Scene:

—Encourage a creative picture or series of pictures.

—Review the setting. Recall the different scenes of the story by asking what the scene looked like, expressions, moods, etc.
  (Example: 1) Jesus leaving the people on shore, 2) Jesus asleep in the boat, 3) Jesus awake and calming the sea)

—Show them the picture from a children's Bible, or

—Put the scene on an overhead projector, or chalk the scene on the board.

Create the Mood:

—As the materials are being passed out have slow, instrumental music playing in the background. (If music was used for "Telling the Story" use the same composition during the art for that Unit.)
  At the same time it might be helpful to have one or two children reread the Gospel text.

—Remind them to share their ideas with others.

Materials:

—Ask the children to take out their pencil and crayons (they may have felt markers, or you may have another medium planned—water color, etc.).

—Pass out the paper.

Appreciation:

—Walk around to look at the work—encourage, offer help if needed, etc.

—Admire their finished product (sometimes hold it up, or let the child walk around and show it).

Folder:

—If possible have the children keep a Gospel folder for their pictures, plays, etc. Let them take the pictures home to show, if they wish, but encourage their return, as they will be useful during the Reflection.

ALTERNATIVES:
—Group work—give out large paper (brown roll paper, primary drawing paper, or tape smaller pieces together) and let groups of children work on different scenes.
—Make a banner (material or paper) for classroom or Eucharistic Celebration, or small ones for their rooms at home.
—Make puppet characters that can be used with play script. Some might work on scenery for the puppet play.
—Opaque projector work—reproducing Gospel scene with felt markers.
—Cut out-stand up figures in a 3-D scene.
—Symbol art, etc.
—Offer a ditto copy of a picture for those who wish to color it or use it as a model in drawing their own picture.

Section C—THE PLAY

1) GENERAL THEORY:
Every child loves to act. Most have recently left the "just pretend" stage. Now, to be involved in a Gospel play is pure joy. They easily identify with the characters as they act out the episode. During production the interaction with fellow actors fosters lessons in sharing, listening, appreciation, team work and, yes, reconciliation.

2) PROCEDURE:
Organization:
—Pass out a ditto copy of the play to each one.
   Ask them to put their name on it and look it over. If the script is difficult, read it over together. (A quick way: divide the class into two groups and let them alternate reading the parts.)
   Tell them they need not memorize their parts for the play.

—**Choosing Groups:**
   Every child has a part in the play. Divide the class into groups according to the number of characters in the performance. The method of grouping could vary for each play—sometimes the children choose their co-actors (risky), or the teacher quickly counts off groups by seating order, or by alphabetical order, or by birthdates, etc. If an odd number is left over after grouping they have the privilege of taking two parts, or "borrowing-an-actor" from another group at the time they perform, or joining other groups to choral-speak with the narrator.

—**Choosing the Cast:**
   The members of each group choose their part in the play. Another way is for the teacher to write the names of the characters on slips of paper and let the members of the group draw them. In this case they sometimes agree to switch around with each other.

—**Practice Time:**
   The groups go to different areas of the room to practice the introduction of the cast, act out their parts, and decide on movements and stage plans. This process will take at least twenty minutes. Costumes and props are optional. Usually they are happy using their imagination.

—**Order of Performance:**
   Forestall the rush to be "first-performers" by drawing for their place in the performance order. Number as many slips of paper as there are groups. Pass around to the groups as they begin their practice and let one member draw for that group's place in the lineup.

—**Final Production:**
   When all groups seem to be ready, call for the performance to begin. All groups sit and watch quietly as one group after the other performs.

3) ALTERNATIVES:

A simple play is always good but often the children appreciate a change. Ask them what they would like.

—Let them make up and write their own script.

—Give a puppet show, either using teacher's script or their own. (In this case prepare puppets during Art period.)

—Give one class play with everyone taking part. There could be choral speaking, and singing added—costumes, scenery, etc.

Section D—REFLECTION

1) GENERAL THEORY:

Every process of learning needs reflection and evaluation. This is a quiet time of recognition and discovery. As the children reflect on their Gospel experiences they realize the message is for them. They are the object of this marvelous love—a personal gift that is always theirs. At the same time they are evaluating their lives, recognizing those areas where they fail to live Gospel values. In this process dialogue is an important channel for self-revelation.

2) PROCEDURE:

Set the Scene:

—Ask the children to take out the pictures they did on the Unit, or

—Hang up the large scenes that the groups worked on together.

—Give a three-point "Review Meditation" on the Gospel. (Example: "Close your eyes, and in your mind fill in the details. You are with Jesus as he walks the road from Samaria to Galilee . . . *pause* . . . Some men are calling out for help and Jesus turns to them . . . *pause* . . . One, a Samaritan, returns to thank Jesus." These meditations can be read by one of the children. Then go on to the questions.

Methods for Asking the Questions:

—Read the questions one by one and call on anyone who is ready to answer. Even if the answer is adequate, ask if anyone has a comment to add before moving to the next question.

—Write question by question on the board, or have individual questions posted on newsprint.

—Pass out a ditto paper with the questions and ask for a few minutes of quiet reflection before asking for answers. Or let them form small groups to discuss question by question. Encourage this kind of sharing since more can participate. Ask them to choose a secretary to take notes and report back for the group at the final session.

—Write out answers to questions. Here, avoid the "Test Question" atmosphere. Writing helps many to be more definite. Let them read their answers to the class or share in small groups.

Prayer:

—This small meditation follows the questions. If possible, keep it for the end of the class period.

—Introduction:

This sets the mood. It is always the same except for the last sentence which contains the theme word.

Teacher: "CLOSE YOUR EYES WHILE WE TALK TO JESUS. HE IS HERE WITH US. HE LISTENS TO OUR PRAYER. HE TELLS US TO HAVE *FAITH*."

Then after assuming the gesture indicated by number, the teacher says, "Repeat after me," and starts the prayer.

—Recitation:
The prayer is set up for an easy line-by-line repetition. The teacher says a line, the children repeat it, etc. Sometimes substitute the repetition with a simple reading of the prayer by the teacher, a child, or a group of children.

Note Book:
—Encourage the children to keep a "Meditation" note book. They enjoy writing their responses, prayers, reflections, etc.

Music:
—At reflection moments, play background music for association, and to help set the tone and mood.

3) ALTERNATIVES:
—Have the children write their own questions. (Example: What questions would you ask Jesus if he came to your house for supper tonight? Or: What questions would Jesus ask you if you were present at this Gospel scene?)
—Role play situations that show the values Jesus gave here. (Example: Actions that show trust, or forgiveness, or gratitude, etc.)
—For a Gospel on thanksgiving or gratitude: "List three gifts God has given you, and share that list with your fellow classmates.
—Write a prayer or a poem in connection with the message of Jesus.
—Draw a picture of you sitting under a tree as you reflect on this Gospel scene. Share your thought. Then hang the picture in your room to remind you of the message Jesus gave you today.

TIME ALLOTMENT

This time chart is an approximate gauge and will vary according to teacher presentation, adaptations, etc. Again, it is important to be flexible, and never hold rigidly to a time pattern.

Sections of a Unit	Approximate Time	Comment
Section A **TELLING THE STORY**	12-14 min.	This includes the preparation and recitation.
Section B **ART FORM**	20-25 min.	Time depends on medium used.
Section C **THE PLAY**	15-20 min. 5-7 min.	Organization and Practice Presentation of one play for a class of thirty with six groups—Approx. sixty min. for Section C).
Section D **REFLECTION**	20-25 min.	Depends on length of discussion. There's better coverage with small groups.

CCD Program:

The coverage of a Unit depends on the teacher and the circumstances.
  —**PLAN 1.**—Divide one Unit over a two week period. 1st week: work through Sections A, B, and organization and practice for Section C. 2nd week: Section C—presentation of plays, and Section D.
  —**PLAN 2.**—Cover one Unit in one session (see adaptations below).

Examples of Adaptations:
—Presentation of a Unit in one session—highlighting SECTION C.
  Section A—Teacher presents the story in simple story form (10 min.).
  Sections B and C—Skills are unified to put the focus on THE PLAY. One play is to be presented. Class is divided into groups of actors, writers (if you want the script changed—e.g., made into three acts, etc.), scenery artists, choral speakers, singers (guitar players, etc.). Together they create a master production to be presented for the Liturgy, parents, or other groups (50 min.).
  Section D—Some conclusions on the sharing of talents (7 min.).
—Presentation of a Unit in one session—highlighting SECTION B.
  Section A—Usual presentation (14 min.).
  Section B—Most of the session is used for well-made banners. This could be group work on several pieces for a special Liturgy. Tie in the gospel of Section A (45 min.). (Omit Section C.)
  Section D—Brief answering of questions stressing Gospel facts (10 min.).
—During Lent highlight Section D—REFLECTIONS with a mini-retreat. Again, focus on Section B with a PUPPET PLAY.

School Program:
One Unit fits easily into a weekly Religion Program. The length of the class periods isn't important since the Sections can be subdivided and continued in the next session. (Example: All the play groups need not perform on one day. Also, art work can be started one day and finished the next.) The adaptations above can be used just as easily for the weekly program as for the CCD sessions.

KEY for GESTURES
and
GEOGRAPHICAL
DIRECTIONS

KEY to GEOGRAPHICAL DIRECTIONS

(+ N) = **North:** GALILEE, NAZARETH, SEA OF TIBERIAS, CANA, etc.

As the teacher faces the children the gesture is made to the LEFT.

(+ S) = **South:** JUDEA, JERUSALEM, BETHLEHEM, etc.

As the teacher faces the children the gesture is made to the RIGHT.

(+ E) = **East:** DESERT (Jordan), EXILE, TERRITORY OF THE WISE MEN

As the teacher faces the children the gesture is made STRAIGHT AHEAD toward the children (indicate the area behind them).

(+ W) = **West:** SAMARIA, EGYPT, ALL NATIONS (that are not Israel)

As the teacher faces the children the gesture is made to the area directly BEHIND (toward wall behind teacher).

KEY FOR GESTURES

No.	GESTURE	REPRESENTATION and DESCRIPTION
1.		WOMAN (wife, mother, girl, Mary, Elizabeth, etc.)
		one hand crossed over the other, about "reading" distance away
2.		MAN (husband, son, boy, Joseph, Zechariah, etc.)
		arms crossed, standing straght
3.		CHILD (infant, baby, etc.)
		arms in cradle position
4.		KING (David, Herod, Pharaoh, ruler, etc.)
		palms of hands on temples, fingers straight up but arched outward
5.		SHEPHERD, ANGER
		clenched fist (as if leaning on staff for shepherd)
6.		DESCENDANT, ANCESTOR, COMING, POINT OUT, ASCENDING, DESCENDING, JERUSALEM
		right hand held high, left hand low forming a diagonal line; eyes move from one hand to the other to indicate direction

No.	GESTURE	REPRESENTATION AND DESCRIPTION
7.		RELATIVE, NEIGHBOR, FRIEND, MULTITUDE, CROWD, NATION, ISRAEL, GATHER, PREACH
		hands out straight to side—turn head from one side-profile to the other
8.		GOD, FATHER, PRAISE, HONOR, LOVE, THANKSGIVING, COMING OF THE MESSIAH, etc.
		arms and hands straight up—palms slightly cupped
9.		HOLY SPIRIT, PRIEST, PRAYER-PETITION, BLESSED
		elbows close to sides, forearms vertical, hands cupped as if holding a ball
10.		JESUS, THE SAVIOR, CHRIST, REDEEM, RESIGNED, WELCOMED
		arms straight out—slightly to side, palms up as if gathering all in welcome
11.		BAPTIZE, DRAW OUT WATER, GROW, SPRING UP, ACCEPT
		extend arm straight forward and turn hand as if pouring water from a shell
12.		ANOINTING, HEALING, POWER
		arms outstretched and slightly raised with hands together, palms down (imposition)

No.	GESTURE	REPRESENTATION AND DESCRIPTION
13.		ANGEL, MESSAGE FROM GOD, VISION PROPHET
		arms straight forward, slanted up, hands vertical with palms out
14.		DECREE, A SCROLL
		arms straight out with clenched fists—one up and one down as if holding an open scroll
15.		SIGN, WORD, WAIT, LISTEN, COMMAND, *POINT OUT
		index finger of right hand held up *straighten arm and point
16.		OFFER, GIVE, SERVE, GREET, CARRY, WORSHIP
		hands together and cupped in offering
17.		NAME, PROCLAIM, WISDOM, FEAST, REVERENCE, etc.
		both hands flat against shoulders with palms out
18.		OLD, SICK, PARALYZED, BURDENED, OPPRESSED, SUBMISSIVE, HUMBLE
		body slightly bent forward, elbows close to body, forearms turned up with finger tips touching shoulders

10

No.	GESTURE	REPRESENTATION AND DESCRIPTION
19.		STAND BESIDE, STAY, REFLECT, *OBEY, FOLLOW ALONG
		arms straight to side with head turned profile *hands locked behind back
20.		THINK, QUESTION, REMEMBER, WONDER, SURPRISE, DREAM
		one hand to side of head
21.		SEE, LOOK, LOOK FORWARD TO, etc.
		hand bent, fingers horizontal over eyebrows
22.		HEAR, LISTEN, etc.
		hand cupped behind ear
23.		SPEAK, EXCLAIM, GREET BY WORD, SHARE, EAT, ASK, TELL, FORETELL
		palm of one hand very close to chin with fingers extending out
24.		CALL, SHOUT, LAUGH, or AN ASIDE (secretly)
		cup one hand close to mouth

No.	GESTURE	REPRESENTATION AND DESCRIPTION
25.		WRITE, REGISTER, COUNT OUT hand in writing position as if holding pen or chalk
26.		GO, WALK, PASS, CLIMB, RUN, VISIT, *OR* RETURN, COME BACK, etc. one hand over the other in circular motion away from body—reverse motion for come or return
27.		LAY, RECLINE, PUT, REST, SLEEP, DIE, BURY, FIX, CLEAN slowly lower outstretched hands as if lowering something to the ground
28.		WAIT, EXPECT, etc. one hand on hip
29.		FEAR, TERRIFIED, AFRAID, SAD, EMBARRASSED, TIRED, DEAD back of hand over eyes
30.		REPENT, SORROW FOR SIN, MOURNING closed fist on chest

UNIT I

THE BIRTH OF JOHN THE BAPTIST IS FORETOLD

UNIT 1—THE BIRTH OF JOHN THE BAPTIST IS FORETOLD

Section A—Telling the story

Background: Priestly role in the Old Testament
Temple
Holy place in the temple
Incense
John, a cousin of Jesus
Angel—messenger of God

Introduction: Today we will tell the story of Zechariah and the visit he had from God's messenger. This John, who is to come, will prepare the way for Jesus.

Now repeat after me:

During the time when Herod was **King** of Judea, (4)
there was a **priest** named Zechariah . . . (9)
His **wife's** name was Elizabeth . . . (1)
They both lived **good lives** in God's sight, (8)
and obeyed fully the Lord's **commandments** . . . (15)
They had no **children** . . . and were both very **old**. (3, 18)

One day Zechariah was . . . taking his turn in daily **service**. . . . (16)
So he went into the **temple** of the Lord, (6)
while the crowd of people outside **prayed** (9)
during the hour of **burning the incense**. (12)

An **angel of the Lord** appeared to him, (13)
standing at the **right side** of the altar. . . . (19)

The angel said to him;
"Don't be afraid, Zechariah.
God has heard your prayer, ⎫ (13)
and your wife Elizabeth will bear you a son. ⎭
You are to **name** him John . . . (15)
From his birth he will be filled with the Holy Spirit. . . . ⎫ (13)
He will get the Lord's people ready for him." ⎭

Zechariah **said** to the angel, (19)
"How shall I know if this is so? (20)
I am an **old** man and my wife also is **old**." (18)

"I am Gabriel," the angel answered.
"I stand in the presence of God, ⎫
who sent me . . . to tell you this good news. . . . ⎬ (13)
Because you have not believed ⎪
you will be unable to speak . . . ⎪
until the day my promise to you comes true." ⎭

In the meantime the people were **waiting** for Zechariah. . . . (28)
When he came out he could not **speak** to them (17)
so they knew he had seen a **vision**. . . . (13)

When his **service** in the temple was over . . . (16)
Zechariah **went** back home. . . . (26)
Later his **wife** Elizabeth became pregnant. . . . (1)
"Now at last the **Lord** has helped me in this way," she said. (8)

Luke 1,5-25

14

UNIT 1—THE BIRTH OF JOHN THE BAPTIST IS FORETOLD

Section B—Art Form

PROCEDURE:

Set the Scene:
—Encourage a creative picture or series of pictures.
—Review the setting. Recall the different scenes of the story by asking what people were there, what the scene looked like, expressions, moods, etc.
—Show a picture from a children's Bible, or
—Put the scene on an overhead transparency or chalk the scene on the board.

Create the Mood:
—As the materials are being passed out have slow, instrumental music playing in the background. (If music was used for "Telling the Story" use the same composition during the art.)
At the same time it might be helpful to have one or two children reread the Gospel text.
—Remind them to share their ideas with others.

Materials:
—Ask the children to take out whatever materials are needed—crayons, felt markers, water colors etc.
—Pass out the paper.

Appreciation:
—Walk around to look at the work—encourage, offer help if needed, etc.
—Admire their finished product (sometimes hold it up, or let the child walk around and show it).

Folder:
If possible have the children keep a Gospel folder for their pictures, plays, etc. Let them take the pictures home to show, if they wish, but encourage their return, as they will be useful during the Reflection.

ALTERNATIVES:
—Group work—give out large paper (brown roll paper, primary drawing paper, or smaller pieces taped together) and let groups of children work on different scenes.
—Make a banner (cloth or paper) for classroom or Eucharistic Celebration, or small ones for their rooms at home.
—Make puppet characters that can be used with play script. Some might work on scenery for the puppet play.
—Opaque projector work, reproducing Gospel scene with felt markers.
—Cut out stand-up figures in a 3-D scene.
—Symbol art, etc.
—Offer a ditto copy of a picture for those who wish to color it or use it as a model in drawing their own picture.

UNIT 1—THE BIRTH OF JOHN THE BAPTIST IS FORETOLD

Section C—The Play

Characters: Narrator 2, Gabriel, Zechariah, Persons 1, 2, 3, 4, Elizabeth, Narrator 1

Narrator 1:   The title of our play is:
THE BIRTH OF JOHN THE BAPTIST IS FORETOLD
(Introduction of characters)

Narrator 2:   During the time when Herod was King of Judea, there was a priest named Zechariah . . . His wife's name was Elizabeth. . . . They both lived good lives in God's sight, and obeyed fully all the Lord's commandments and rules. They had no children . . . and . . . were both very old.   (Luke 1, 5-7)

Narrator 1:   One day Zechariah was doing his work as a priest before God, taking his turn in the daily service. . . . He went into the temple of the Lord, while the crowd of people outside prayed during the hour of burning the incense.
(Luke 1, 8-10)

Narrator 2:   An angel of the Lord appeared to him, standing at the right side of the altar. . . . When Zechariah saw him he was troubled and felt afraid.
(Luke 1, 11-12)

Gabriel: Don't be afraid, Zechariah! God has heard your prayer, and your wife Elizabeth will bear you a son. You are to name him John. How glad . . . you will be . . . when he is born! For he will be a great man in the Lord's sight. . . . From his very birth he will be filled with the Holy Spirit. He will bring back the people of Israel to the Lord their God. . . . He will get the Lord's people ready for him.   (Luke 1, 13-17)

Zechariah: How shall I know if this is so? I am an old man and my wife is also old.
(Luke 1, 18)

Gabriel: I am Gabriel. . . . I stand in the presence of God, who sent me to speak to you and tell you this good news. . . . Because you have not believed you will be unable to speak . . . until the day my promise to you comes true.''
(Luke 1, 19-20)

Person 1:   Where is Zechariah?
Person 2:   Why doesn't he come out?
Person 3:   He has been in the holy place for so long!

(Zechariah comes out and stands before the people, making signs that he cannot speak and motioning toward heaven.)

Person 4:   He has seen a vision in the temple!

Elizabeth: The Lord has done this for me. He is going to give me a child! Praise the name of the Lord!

UNIT 1—THE BIRTH OF JOHN THE BAPTIST IS FORETOLD

Section D—REFLECTION

Questions:

That day, when Zechariah walked into the temple to pray for the people, he had no idea that a big announcement was coming.

1. What was the message of God that the angel brought Zechariah?
2. How did Zechariah respond to that word of God?
3. How did God show Zechariah that he should be more trusting?
4. What does it mean to be "trust-worthy"?
5. When do you put your trust in others? Give examples.
6. When do your parents put their trust in you?
7. What are some ways of building another's trust, or becoming a "trust-worthy" person? (Do a job well, be truthful, don't exaggerate, etc.)

Prayer:

Close your eyes while we talk to Jesus. He is here with us. He listens to our prayer. He shows us how to TRUST in him. Repeat after me. (16)

> LORD JESUS,
> YOU ARE MY GOD.
> I AM YOUR CHILD.
> YOU GIVE ME YOUR LOVE.
> YOU TRUST ME TO SHOW OTHERS YOUR LOVE.
> I NEED YOUR HELP.
> THANK YOU, JESUS.
> AMEN.

UNIT 2

THE BIRTH OF JESUS IS ANNOUNCED

UNIT 2—THE BIRTH OF JESUS IS ANNOUNCED

Section A—Telling the Story

Background: Mary (other names for Mary: Mother of Jesus, Mother of God, etc.)
King David (King of Israel and Judah about a thousand years before Christ)
Nazareth

Introduction: Today we will talk about that special person named Mary. Just six months after Gabriel visited Zechariah to announce John's coming, God sent the same messenger to Mary with even greater news—the good news everyone was waiting for.

Repeat after me.

God sent the **angel Gabriel** (13)
to a town in Galilee named *Nazareth. (*N)

He had a message for a **girl**, (1)
promised in marriage to . . . **Joseph**, (2)
who was a **descendant** of **King David.** (6, 4)
The girl's name was **Mary.** (9)

The angel came to her and said, "Peace be with you!
The Lord is with you, and has greatly **blessed** you!" (13)
Mary was troubled . . . and **wondered** what his words meant. (20)

The angel said to her,
"**Don't be afraid**, Mary. God has been gracious to you. . . . (13)
You will give birth to a **son**, (3)
and you will name him **Jesus**. (10)

19

He will be **great**, (8)
and will be called **Son of the Most High God**. (10)
The Lord God will make him a king, as his **ancestor** David was, (6)
and he will be king of the **descendants** of Jacob forever; (6)
his **kingdom will never end**." (17)

Mary said . . . "How can this be?" (1)
The angel answered: (13)
"The **Holy Spirit** will come on you, (9)
and **God's power** will rest upon you. (12)
For this reason the **holy child** will be called the Son of God. . . . (8)
Remember your **relative** Elizabeth. . . . (7)
She is now six months pregnant, (1)
even though she is very **old**. (18)
For there is **not a thing** that **God** cannot do." (15, 8)

"**I am the Lord's servant**," said Mary; (17)
"**may it happen to me as you have said**." (16)
And the angel left **her**. (1)

UNIT 1—THE BIRTH OF JOHN THE BAPTIST IS FORETOLD

Section B—Art Form

PROCEDURE:

Set the Scene:
—Encourage a creative picture or series of pictures.
—Review the setting. Recall the different scenes of the story by asking what people were
  there, what the scene looked like, expressions, moods, etc.
—Show a picture from a children's Bible, or
—Put the scene on an overhead transparency or chalk the scene on the board.

Create the Mood:
—As the materials are being passed out have slow, instrumental music playing in the
  background. (If music was used for "Telling the Story" use the same composition
  during the art.)
  At the same time it might be helpful to have one or two children reread the Gospel text.
—Remind them to share their ideas with others.

Materials:
—Ask the children to take out whatever materials are needed—crayons, felt markers,
  water colors etc.
—Pass out the paper.

Appreciation:
—Walk around to look at the work—encourage, offer help if needed, etc.
—Admire their finished product (sometimes hold it up, or let the child walk around and
  show it).

Folder:
  If possible have the children keep a Gospel folder for their pictures, plays, etc. Let them
  take the pictures home to show, if they wish, but encourage their return, as they will be
  useful during the Reflection.

ALTERNATIVES:

—Group work—give out large paper (brown roll paper, primary drawing paper, or smaller pieces taped together) and let groups of children work on different scenes.

—Make a banner (cloth or paper) for classroom or Eucharistic Celebration, or small ones for their rooms at home.

—Make puppet characters that can be used with play script. Some might work on scenery for the puppet play.

—Opaque projector work, reproducing Gospel scene with felt markers.

—Cut out stand-up figures in a 3-D scene.

—Symbol art, etc.

—Offer a ditto copy of a picture for those who wish to color it or use it as a model in drawing their own picture.

UNIT 2—THE BIRTH OF JESUS IS ANNOUNCED

Section C—The Play

Characters: Group, Gabriel, Mary, Narrator

Narrator:
The title of our play is:
THE BIRTH OF JESUS IS ANNOUNCED
(Introduction of characters)

This scene takes place six months after the angel Gabriel had announced the coming of John to Zechariah and Elizabeth.

Group:
In the sixth month . . . God sent the angel Gabriel to a town in Galilee named Nazareth. He had a message for a girl promised in marriage to a man named Joseph, who was a descendant of King David. The girl's name was Mary.
(Luke 1, 26-27)

Gabriel:
Peace be with you! The Lord is with you, and has greatly blessed you!
(Luke 1, 28)

Group:
Mary was deeply troubled by the angel's message, and she wondered what the words meant.
(Luke 1, 29)

Gabriel:
Don't be afraid, Mary, for God has been gracious to you. You will . . . give birth to a son, and you will name him Jesus. He will be great and will be called the son of the Most High God. The Lord God will make him a king, as his ancestor David was, and he will be the king of the descendants of Jacob forever; his kingdom will never end!
(Luke 1, 30-33)

Mary:
How . . . can this be?
(Luke 1, 34)

Gabriel:
The Holy Spirit will come on you, and God's power will rest upon you. For this reason the holy child will be called the Son of God. Remember your cousin Elizabeth. . . . She herself is now six months pregnant, even though she is very old. For there is not a thing that God cannot do. (Luke 1, 35-37)

Mary:
I am the Lord's servant. . . . May it happen to me as you have said.
(Luke 1, 38)

Group:
And then the messenger of God left Mary.

UNIT 2—THE BIRTH OF JESUS IS ANNOUNCED

Section D—REFLECTION

Questions:

Remember that this was a great moment for Mary and for the world. Let's think about the things Mary heard and said that day.

1. What did Gabriel mean by saying Mary was blessed among all women?
2. How did Mary tell God that she wanted to do his will?
3. Why do you think that Mary was ready to say "yes" to what God was asking?
4. What other good news did the angel have to share with Mary?
5. What were some of the hard things Mary had to face in accepting God's plan?
6. What kind of an act does it take to say "yes" to something we know will be hard?
7. Can you remember a time when you had a choice of saying "yes" or "no." What happened?

Prayer:

Close your eyes while we talk to Jesus. He is here with us. He listens to our prayer. He helps us to ACCEPT HIS WILL. Repeat after me. (16)

> LORD JESUS,
> YOU WANTED MARY TO BE YOUR MOTHER,
> AND SHE SAID "YES."
> THAT MEANS SHE IS MY MOTHER TOO.
> TEACH ME HOW TO SAY,
> "MARY, MOTHER OF JESUS AND MY MOTHER,
> HELP ME SAY 'YES' TO JESUS."
> AMEN.

UNIT 3

MARY VISITS ELIZABETH

UNIT 3—MARY VISITS ELIZABETH

Section A—Telling the Story

Background: Mary's hymn of praise (Jewish tradition)

Introduction: After the angel left, Mary went to visit Elizabeth. This is what happened.

Repeat after me.

Mary . . . **hurried off** to a hill country to a town in *Judea. (26, *S)
She **went** into Zechariah's house and **greeted** Elizabeth. . . . (26, 16)

Elizabeth was filled with the **Holy Spirit**, (9)
and **spoke** in a loud voice: (23)
"Blessed are you among women,
and blessed is the child you will bear!
Why should this great thing happen to me,
that my Lord's mother comes to visit me? . . .
How happy are you to believe the Lord's message to you. . . ." } (9)

Mary **said**: (23)
"My heart praises the Lord.
My soul is glad because of God my Savior.
For he has remembered me, his lowly servant! } (17)

And from now on all people will call me blessed.
Because of the great things the Mighty God has done for me,
his name is holy;
He shows mercy . . . from one generation to another. . . . } (8)

He . . . scattered the proud people,
he brought down mighty kings . . .
and lifted up the lowly.
He filled the hungry with good things,
and sent the rich away with empty hands. } (6)

He kept the promise . . . to help his servant Israel
and remembered to show mercy to Abraham,
and to all his descendants for ever. } (9)

Mary **stayed** about three months with Elizabeth, (19)
and then **went** back home. (26)

Luke 1, 39-56

UNIT 3—MARY VISITS ELIZABETH

Section B—Art Form

PROCEDURE:

Set the Scene:
—Encourage a creative picture or series of pictures.
—Review the setting. Recall the different scenes of the story by asking what people were there, what the scene looked like, expressions, moods, etc.
—Show a picture from a children's Bible, or
—Put the scene on an overhead transparency or chalk the scene on the board.

Create the Mood:
—As the materials are being passed out have slow, instrumental music playing in the background. (If music was used for "Telling the Story" use the same composition during the art.)
At the same time it might be helpful to have one or two children reread the Gospel text.
—Remind them to share their ideas with others.

Materials:
—Ask the children to take out whatever materials are needed—crayons, felt markers, water colors etc.
—Pass out the paper.

Appreciation:
—Walk around to look at the work—encourage, offer help if needed, etc.
—Admire their finished product (sometimes hold it up, or let the child walk around and show it).

Folder:
If possible have the children keep a Gospel folder for their pictures, plays, etc. Let them take the pictures home to show, if they wish, but encourage their return, as they will be useful during the Reflection.

ALTERNATIVES:
—Group work—give out large paper (brown roll paper, primary drawing paper, or smaller pieces taped together) and let groups of children work on different scenes.
—Make a banner (cloth or paper) for classroom or Eucharistic Celebration, or small ones for their rooms at home.
—Make puppet characters that can be used with play script. Some might work on scenery for the puppet play.
—Opaque projector work, reproducing Gospel scene with felt markers.
—Cut out stand-up figures in a 3-D scene.
—Symbol art, etc.
—Offer a ditto copy of a picture for those who wish to color it or use it as a model in drawing their own picture.

UNIT 3—MARY VISITS ELIZABETH

Section C—The Play

Characters: Narrator 2, Elizabeth, Mary, Narrator 1.

Narrator 1:   The title of our story is:
MARY VISITS ELIZABETH
(introduction of characters)

Narrator 2:   Our play takes place just after the angel Gabriel left Mary, having told her that she would be the mother of Jesus.

Narrator 1:   Mary got ready and hurried off to the hill country, to a town in Judea. She went into Zechariah's house and greeted Elizabeth. When Elizabeth heard Mary's greeting . . . Elizabeth was filled with the Holy Spirit. . . .

(Luke 1, 39-41)

Elizabeth: Blessed are you among women! Blessed is the child you will bear! Why should this great thing happen to me, that my Lord's mother comes to visit me? How happy are you to believe that the Lord's message to you will come true.

(Luke 1, 42-45)

(soft background music for:)

Mary: My heart praises the Lord.
My soul is glad because of God my Savior.
For he has remembered me, his lowly servant.
And from now on all people will call me blessed.
Because of the great things the Mighty God has done for me,
His name is holy.
He shows mercy . . . from one generation to another. . . .
He brought down mighty kings . . . and lifted up the lowly. . . .
He kept the promise . . . to help his servant Israel
and remembered to show mercy to Abraham,
and to all his descendants for ever.

(Luke 1, 46-50, 52, 54, 55)

Narrators
1 and 2:   Mary stayed about three months with Elizabeth, and then went back home.

(Luke 1, 56)

UNIT 3—MARY VISITS ELIZABETH

Section D—REFLECTION

Questions:

God's gift to Mary was the greatest gift ever received. That gift of Jesus was to be shared with everyone.

1. Why did Mary go off to visit Elizabeth?
2. Who told Elizabeth about Mary's great blessing?
3. What did Mary say to praise God for her good news?
4. Then what did Mary do to show Elizabeth that she really cared about her?
5. When something good is happening to us, do we usually think about others? Why not?
6. Is it easy for you to share the joy or good news of another?
7. What kind of gifts has God given you? Can you share them with others? How?

Prayer:

Close your eyes while we talk to Jesus. He is here with us. He listens to our prayer. He wants us to be CARING people. Repeat after me. (16)

> LORD JESUS,
> MARY CARED ABOUT ELIZABETH.
> SHE STAYED TO HELP.
> I CARE ABOUT MY FAMILY.
> SHOW ME HOW TO HELP.
> TEACH ME HOW TO LOVE.
> THANK YOU, JESUS.
> AMEN.

UNIT 4

THE BIRTH OF JOHN THE BAPTIST

UNIT 4—THE BIRTH OF JOHN THE BAPTIST

Section A—Telling the Story

Background: Circumcision—sign of God's covenant.

Introduction: Zechariah had not been able to speak for nine months because he had not believed God's messenger. Now it is time for Elizabeth to have her child. Here is what happened.

Repeat after me.

The time came for **Elizabeth** to have her baby, (1)
and she gave birth to a **son**. (3)
The **neighbors and relatives heard** how good the Lord had been to her, (7, 22)
and they all **rejoiced** with her. (8)

When the **baby** was a week old, } (3)
they came to circumcise him.
They were going to **name** him Zechariah, his father's name. (17)
But his mother said,
"**No**! His **name** will be John." (15, 17)

They **said** to her, (23)
"But you don't have a single **relative** with that name." (7)
Then they made a **sign** to his father, (16)
asking what **name** he would like the boy to have. (17)

Zechariah asked for a writing pad and **wrote**, (25)
"**His name is John**." (25)
How **surprised** they all were! (20)

At that moment Zechariah was able to **speak** again, (23)
and he started **praising** God. (8)
The neighbors were filled with **fear**. (29)

News about these things **spread** throughout the hill country. . . . (7)
All who heard of it . . . **asked**, (20)
''What is this **child** going to be?'' (3)
For it was plain that the Lord's **power** was with him. . . . (12)

The child **grew** . . . in body and spirit. (11)
He lived in the **desert** (21)
until the day when he would appear **publicly** (7)
to the people of Israel. (7)

Luke 1, 57-66, 80

UNIT 4—THE BIRTH OF JOHN THE BAPTIST

Section B—Art Form

PROCEDURE:

Set the Scene:
—Encourage a creative picture or series of pictures.
—Review the setting. Recall the different scenes of the story by asking what people were there, what the scene looked like, expressions, moods, etc.
—Show a picture from a children's Bible, or
—Put the scene on an overhead transparency or chalk the scene on the board.

Create the Mood:
—As the materials are being passed out have slow, instrumental music playing in the background. (If music was used for "Telling the Story" use the same composition during the art.)
   At the same time it might be helpful to have one or two children reread the Gospel text.
—Remind them to share their ideas with others.

Materials:
—Ask the children to take out whatever materials are needed—crayons, felt markers, water colors etc.
—Pass out the paper.

Appreciation:
—Walk around to look at the work—encourage, offer help if needed, etc.
—Admire their finished product (sometimes hold it up, or let the child walk around and show it).

Folder:
   If possible have the children keep a Gospel folder for their pictures, plays, etc. Let them take the pictures home to show, if they wish, but encourage their return, as they will be useful during the Reflection.

ALTERNATIVES:
—Group work—give out large paper (brown roll paper, primary drawing paper, or smaller pieces taped together) and let groups of children work on different scenes.
—Make a banner (cloth or paper) for classroom or Eucharistic Celebration, or small ones for their rooms at home.
—Make puppet characters that can be used with play script. Some might work on scenery for the puppet play.
—Opaque projector work, reproducing Gospel scene with felt markers.
—Cut out stand-up figures in a 3-D scene.
—Symbol art, etc.
—Offer a ditto copy of a picture for those who wish to color it or use it as a model in drawing their own picture.

UNIT 4—THE BIRTH OF JOHN THE BAPTIST

Section C—The Play

Characters: Narrator 2, Relative 1, 2, Neighbor, Elizabeth, Zechariah, Narrator 1.

Narrator 1:	The title of the play is: **THE BIRTH OF JOHN THE BAPTIST** (Introduction of characters)
Narrator 2:	The time came for Elizabeth to have her baby, and she gave birth to a son. Her neighbors and relatives heard how . . . good the Lord had been to her, and they rejoiced with her. <div align="right">(Luke 1, 57-58)</div>
Relative 1:	Have you heard the latest news? God has blessed our cousin Elizabeth with a baby boy!
Relative 2:	Yes, he is a week old today. We must go and celebrate the circumcision of the child.
Neighbor:	Give glory to God for all he has done! How proud Zechariah must be! Of course the boy will have his father's name.
Elizabeth:	No! His name will be **JOHN**.<div align="right">(Luke 1, 60)</div>
Relative 1:	But you don't have a single relative with that name.<div align="right">(Luke 1, 61)</div>
Relative 2:	Let's ask Zechariah about this. Make him a sign. (Relatives and friends make signs.)
Narrator 1:	(Zechariah motions for tablet, writes and holds up message.) Zechariah asked for a writing pad and wrote "**HIS NAME IS JOHN**."<div align="right">Luke 1, 63)</div>
Narrator 2:	At that moment Zechariah was able to speak again, and he started praising God. . . . Filled with the Holy Spirit he prophesied: (Luke 1, 64, 67)
Zechariah:	(soft music in background) Let us praise the Lord, the God of Israel! For he came to help his people and set them free. . . . You, my child, will be called a prophet of the Most High God. You will go ahead of the Lord to prepare his road for him, to tell the people that they will be saved. . . . For God is merciful and tender; he will cause the bright dawn of salvation to rise on us . . . to guide our steps into the path of peace.<div align="right">(Luke 1, 68, 76-79)</div>
Narrators 1 and 2:	The child grew and developed in body and spirit; he lived in the desert until the day when he would appear publicly to the people of Israel.<div align="right">(Luke 1, 80)</div>

UNIT 4—THE BIRTH OF JOHN THE BAPTIST

Section D—REFLECTION

Questions:

God had greatly blessed Elizabeth and Zechariah with a very special son. From the beginning they knew he had one mission.

1. What name did the relatives want to give Elizabeth's son?
2. When did God keep his promise to Zechariah and show that his lack of trust was forgiven?
3. When Zechariah praised God in prayer, what did he say John's mission would be?
4. John was a leader of men. How was he able to step aside and point the way to Jesus?
5. Do we have a mission to show the way to Jesus? How?
6. Is it easy to step aside and let others be first? Why not?
7. Why is it hard to watch other people win?
8. Can you remember a time when you really tried to be unselfish? What happened?

Prayer:

Close your eyes while we talk to Jesus. He is here with us. He listens to our prayer. He helps us to be UNSELFISH. Repeat after me. (16)

> LORD JESUS,
> YOU ARE MY FATHER.
> YOU WANT MY LOVE TO POINT THE WAY TO YOU.
> WHEN I AM KIND,
> I SAY YOU ARE GOOD.
> WHEN I AM GENEROUS,
> I SAY YOU ARE LOVE.
> WHEN I AM SORRY,
> I SAY YOU FORGIVE.
> LORD JESUS, KEEP ME IN YOUR LOVE.
> AMEN.

UNIT 5

THE BIRTH OF JESUS

UNIT 5—THE BIRTH OF JESUS

Section A—Telling the Story

Background: Register-census
Emperor Caesar Augustus
Cloths (swaddling clothes)
Inn

Introduction: Now the time had come for Mary to bring Jesus into the world. Let's thank God as we tell the story.

Repeat after me.

At that time Emperor Augustus sent out an **order** (14)
for all citizens . . . to **register** . . . for the census. . . . (25)
Joseph **went** . . . to *Judea, to the town named Bethlehem . . . (26, *S)
because he was a **descendant** of **King** David. (6, 4)
He went to register . . . with **Mary**. . . . (1)

While they were in Bethlehem . . .
She **gave birth** to her first son, (3)
wrapped him in cloths, and **laid** him in a manger, (26, 27)
for there was **no room** for them . . . in the inn. (10)

There were **shepherds** . . . in the fields . . . **taking care** of their flocks. (5, 21)
An **angel** of the Lord appeared to them (13)
and the glory of the Lord **shone** over them. . . . (7)

The angel said . . . "Don't be afraid, for I am here with **good news** . . . (8)
which will bring great **joy** to **all** the people. (9, 7)
This very night, in *David's town (*S)
your Savior was **born, Christ the Lord**! (3, 6)
This is what will **prove** it to you. (15)
You will find a **baby wrapped** in cloths and **lying** in a manger." (3, 26, 27)

Suddenly a great **army** of . . . **angels** appeared . . . **singing** praises to God: (7, 13, 24)
"Glory to God in the highest heaven!
And peace on earth to men with whom he is pleased." } (8)

When the angels **went away** . . . the shepherds **said** to one another, (26, 23)
"Let us go to *Bethlehem and see this thing that has happened. . . ." (*S)

So they **hurried off** and found **Mary** and **Joseph**, (26, 1, 2)
and saw the **baby lying** in the manger. . . . (3, 27)
They **told** them what the **angel** had said about this **child**. (23, 13, 3)
All who **heard** it were filled with **wonder**. . . . (22, 20)

Mary remembered all these things and thought deeply about them. (1)
The **shepherds** went back, (5)
singing praises to God for all they had heard and seen; (24)
it had been **just as the angel had told them**. (15)

Luke 2, 1-20

UNIT 5—THE BIRTH OF JESUS

Section B—Art Form

PROCEDURE:

Set the Scene:
—Encourage a creative picture or series of pictures.
—Review the setting. Recall the different scenes of the story by asking what people were there, what the scene looked like, expressions, moods, etc.
—Show a picture from a children's Bible, or
—Put the scene on an overhead transparency or chalk the scene on the board.

Create the Mood:
—As the materials are being passed out have slow, instrumental music playing in the background. (If music was used for "Telling the Story" use the same composition during the art.)
    At the same time it might be helpful to have one or two children reread the Gospel text.
—Remind them to share their ideas with others.

Materials:
—Ask the children to take out whatever materials are needed—crayons, felt markers, water colors etc.
—Pass out the paper.

Appreciation:
—Walk around to look at the work—encourage, offer help if needed, etc.
—Admire their finished product (sometimes hold it up, or let the child walk around and show it).

Folder:
    If possible have the children keep a Gospel folder for their pictures, plays, etc. Let them take the pictures home to show, if they wish, but encourage their return, as they will be useful during the Reflection.

ALTERNATIVES:

—Group work—give out large paper (brown roll paper, primary drawing paper, or smaller pieces taped together) and let groups of children work on different scenes.
—Make a banner (cloth or paper) for classroom or Eucharistic Celebration, or small ones for their rooms at home.
—Make puppet characters that can be used with play script. Some might work on scenery for the puppet play.

—Opaque projector work, reproducing Gospel scene with felt markers.
—Cut out stand-up figures in a 3-D scene.
—Symbol art, etc.
—Offer a ditto copy of a picture for those who wish to color it or use it as a model in drawing their own picture.

UNIT 5—THE BIRTH OF JESUS

Section C—The Play

Characters: Group 1, 2 (tableau scene: Mary, Joseph, the Child), Angel, Shepherds, Narrator.

Narrator: The title of this play is:
THE BIRTH OF JESUS
(Introduction of characters)

Group 1: At that time Emperor Augustus sent out an order for all citizens . . . to register . . . for the census . . . each to his own town. (Luke 2, 1-2)

Group 2: Joseph went from the town of Nazareth in Galilee, to Judea, to the town of Bethlehem, where King David was born . . . because he was a descendant of David. (Luke 2, 4)

Groups 1 and 2: He went with Mary, who was promised in marriage to him. . . . While they were in Bethlehem . . . she gave birth to her first son, wrapped him in cloths and laid him in a manger, for there was no room for them to stay in the inn. (Tableau scene) (Luke 2, 5-7)

Group 1: There were some shepherds in that part of the country . . . spending the night in the fields taking care of their flocks. (Luke 2, 8)

Group 2: An angel of the Lord appeared to them, and the glory of the Lord shone over them. They were terribly afraid. (Luke 2, 9)

Angel: Don't be afraid: For I am here with good news . . . which will bring great joy to all the people. This very night in David's town your Savior was born—Christ the Lord. This is what will prove it to you: You will find a baby wrapped in cloths and lying in a manger. (Luke 2, 10-12)

Narrator: Suddenly a great army of heaven's angels appeared . . . singing praises to God. (Luke 2, 13)

Angel & Groups 1 & 2: Glory to God in the highest heaven! And peace on earth to men with whom he is pleased. (Luke 2, 14)

Shepherd: Let us go to Bethlehem and see this thing that has happened that the Lord has told us. (Shepherds come to tableau) (Luke 2, 15)

Group 1: They hurried off and found Mary and Joseph, and saw the baby lying in the manger. (Luke 2, 16)

Group 2: When the shepherds saw him they told them what the angel had said about this child. All who heard it were filled with wonder. (Luke 2, 17-19)

| Narrator: | Mary remembered all these things, and thought deeply about them. |
| | (Luke 2, 19) |

| Groups 1 and 2: | The shepherds went back singing praises to God for all they had heard and seen; it had been just as the angel had told them. (Luke 2, 20) |

(Suggestion: Use two areas of stage—tableau of Holy Family at one end and shepherds in the field at other.)

UNIT 5—THE BIRTH OF JESUS

Section D—REFLECTION

Questions:

For many centuries the people of Israel had waited for the Savior. They did not know when or how he would come, but they expected him and waited.

1. Why did Mary and Joseph leave their home in Nazareth at this time?
2. Where were they the night Jesus was born?
3. Of all the people in Israel, who were the first ones to know that Jesus had come? Why?
4. What directions did the angel give the shepherds so they would know him?
5. How do you think the shepherds felt about the way everyone was treating them that night?
6. If being loved and cared about makes us feel wanted and "at home," what can we do to make others know we care about them?
7. What are the only directions you would give someone for finding Jesus?

Prayer:

Close your eyes while we talk to Jesus. He is here with us. He listens to our prayer. He wants us to be "AT HOME" with him. Repeat after me. (16)

LORD JESUS,
YOU ARE THE SAVIOR.
YOU ARE EVERYONE'S FRIEND.
LET ME FIND YOU WHEN I HELP THE POOR.
LET ME FIND YOU WHEN I VISIT THE SICK.
LET ME FIND YOU WHEN I LOVE MY ENEMIES.
THANK YOU FOR FINDING ME, JESUS.
AMEN.

UNIT 6

JESUS IS PRESENTED IN THE TEMPLE

UNIT 6—JESUS IS PRESENTED IN THE TEMPLE

Section A—Telling the Story

Introduction: The people of Israel kept certain laws that had been passed down since the time of Moses. One of these laws said that parents should bring their first-born child to the temple to be consecrated to the Lord. They were also to make an offering of a pair of turtle doves or two young pigeons. This is what happened when Jesus was forty days old.

Repeat after me.

Joseph and Mary . . . took the **child** to Jerusalem, (3)
to **present** him to the Lord . . . (11)
and to **offer** a sacrifice . . . as required by the Law . . . (16)

Now there was a **man** living in Jerusalem (2)
whose **name** was Simeon . . . (17)
a good and **God-fearing** man. . . . (9)
He had been **assured** by the Holy Spirit that he would not **die** (15, 27)
before he had seen the Lord's **promised Messiah**. (8)

Led by the Spirit, Simeon **went** into the temple. (26)
When the parents brought the **child Jesus** into the temple . . . (3)
Simeon **took** the child in his arms, (11)
and gave thanks to God:
"NOW, LORD, YOU HAVE KEPT YOUR PROMISE,
AND YOU MAY LET YOUR SERVANT GO IN PEACE.
FOR WITH MY OWN EYES I HAVE SEEN YOUR SALVATION,
WHICH YOU HAVE MADE READY IN THE PRESENCE OF ALL PEOPLES:
A LIGHT TO REVEAL YOUR WAY TO THE GENTILES,
AND TO GIVE GLORY TO YOUR PEOPLE ISRAEL." } (16)

The child's father and mother were **amazed** (20)
at the things Simeon **said** about him. (23)

Simeon **blessed** them and **said** to Mary his mother: (12, 19)
"This child is chosen by God
for the destruction and salvation of many in Israel;
he will be a sign from God
which many people will speak against,   } (17)
and so reveal their secret thoughts.
And sorrow, like a sharp sword,
will break your own heart."

There was a prophetess named **Anna** who . . . never left the temple; (1)
day and night she **worshipped** God, fasting and praying. (16)
That very same hour she **arrived**, gave **thanks** to God, (26, 8)
and **spoke** about the child (23)
to all who were **waiting** for God to **redeem** Jerusalem. (28, 10)

Luke 2, 22-38

UNIT 6—JESUS IS PRESENTED IN THE TEMPLE

Section B—Art Form

PROCEDURE:

Set the Scene:
—Encourage a creative picture or series of pictures.
—Review the setting. Recall the different scenes of the story by asking what people were there, what the scene looked like, expressions, moods, etc.
—Show a picture from a children's Bible, or
—Put the scene on an overhead transparency or chalk the scene on the board.

Create the Mood:
—As the materials are being passed out have slow, instrumental music playing in the background. (If music was used for "Telling the Story" use the same composition during the art.)
  At the same time it might be helpful to have one or two children reread the Gospel text.
—Remind them to share their ideas with others.

Materials:
—Ask the children to take out whatever materials are needed—crayons, felt markers, water colors etc.
—Pass out the paper.

Appreciation:
—Walk around to look at the work—encourage, offer help if needed, etc.
—Admire their finished product (sometimes hold it up, or let the child walk around and show it).

Folder:
  If possible have the children keep a Gospel folder for their pictures, plays, etc. Let them take the pictures home to show, if they wish, but encourage their return, as they will be useful during the Reflection.

ALTERNATIVES:
—Group work—give out large paper (brown roll paper, primary drawing paper, or smaller pieces taped together) and let groups of children work on different scenes.
—Make a banner (cloth or paper) for classroom or Eucharistic Celebration, or small ones for their rooms at home.
—Make puppet characters that can be used with play script. Some might work on scenery for the puppet play.
—Opaque projector work, reproducing Gospel scene with felt markers.
—Cut out stand-up figures in a 3-D scene.
—Symbol art, etc.
—Offer a ditto copy of a picture for those who wish to color it or use it as a model in drawing their own picture.

UNIT 6—JESUS IS PRESENTED IN THE TEMPLE

Section C—The Play

Characters: Group 1, Group 2, Simeon, Mary, Joseph, Anna, Narrator

Narrator: The title of our play is:
JESUS IS PRESENTED IN THE TEMPLE
(Introduction of characters)

When Jesus was forty days old Mary and Joseph took him to the temple in Jerusalem to present him to the Lord.

Group 1:   This is what is written in the Law of the Lord: "Every first-born male shall be dedicated to the Lord." They also went to offer a sacrifice as required by the Law . . . "A pair of doves or two young pigeons."   (Luke 2, 23, 24)

Group 2:   Now there was a man living in Jerusalem whose name was Simeon. He was a good and God-fearing man . . . waiting for Israel to be saved. . . . He had been assured by the Holy Spirit that he would not die before he had seen the Lord's promised Messiah.   (Luke 2, 25, 26)

Narrator: When the parents brought the child Jesus into the temple . . . Simeon took the child into his arms and gave thanks to God: (Luke 2, 27-28)

Simeon: Now, Lord, you have kept your promise,
and you may let your servant go in peace.
For with my own eyes I have seen your salvation,
which you have made ready, in the presence of all peoples:
A light to reveal your way to the Gentiles,
and to give glory to your people Israel.   (Luke 2, 29-32)

Mary: Joseph, I am amazed at the things Simeon said about Jesus! We must thank God as he gives us the blessing.

Joseph: Yes, and now I think he is going to speak to you, Mary.

Simeon: (Simeon turns to Mary)
This child is chosen by God for the destruction and salvation of many in Israel; he will be a sign from God which many people will speak against . . . and sorrow, like a sharp sword, will break your own heart."   (Luke 2, 34-35)

Narrator: There was a prophetess named Anna . . . an old woman. . . . She never left the temple; day and night she worshiped God, fasting and praying. That very hour she arrived at the temple . . . and spoke about the child. . . .
          (Luke 2, 36-38)

Anna: Listen, all you who look for salvation and who wait for God to redeem Jerusalem. Praise the Lord, for he is here with us! Give thanks to God, for he has come to be with his people!

UNIT 6—JESUS IS PRESENTED IN THE TEMPLE

Section D—REFLECTION

Questions:

In this Gospel Jesus is called the "light." How easy it is to find the way when you are sure of the road.

1. What happened when Jesus was forty days old?

2. Who was in the temple at that time, and what do we know about him?

3. What message did God give Simeon about the Saviour?

4. Simeon said some would not follow the "light." What connection did this have with Simeon's message to Mary?

5. How was Jesus a "light" for Simeon and holy Anna?

6. Has anyone ever been a "light" for you? In what way?

7. Have you ever been a "light" for someone else?

8. How can we turn away from the "light"?

Prayer:

Close your eyes while we talk to Jesus. He is here with us. He listens to our prayer. He wants to be a "LIGHT" for us. Repeat after me. (9)

> LORD JESUS,
> KEEP YOUR LIGHT BEFORE ME.
> NEVER LET ME SAY,
> "I HAVEN'T TIME,"
> "IT'S TOO MUCH TROUBLE,"
> "I'LL DO IT LATER."
> HELP ME SAY, "I'M SORRY."
> GUIDE ME, LORD JESUS.
> AMEN.

UNIT 7

THE WISE MEN

UNIT 7—THE WISE MEN

Section A—Telling the Story

Background: Men who studied the stars ('Wise Men')
Prophet
The star

Introduction: St. Matthew tells this story. The tradition of gift-giving at Christmas may have started when the early Christians came together to celebrate this feast.

Repeat after me.

Jesus was born in the town of *Bethlehem (*S)
during the time when **Herod** was king. (4)
Soon afterward some men who studied the **stars** (15)
came from the *east to **Jerusalem**, and asked, (26, *S, 6)
''Where is the **baby** born to be king of the Jews? (3)
We **saw** his star . . . in the east, (21)
and we have come to **worship** him.'' (17)

When King Herod **heard** about this he was **very upset**. (22, 29)
He **called** . . . the chief **priests** (24, 2)
and **teachers** of the law, and asked . . . (14)
''**Where** will the Messiah be born?'' (23)

''In the town of *Bethlehem in Judea,'' they **answered**. . . . (*S, 23)
''The prophet **wrote**: (25)
'YOU, *BETHLEHEM, IN THE LAND OF JUDAH, (*W)
ARE NOT . . . LEAST AMONG THE RULERS OF JUDAH.
FOR FROM YOU WILL COME A LEADER
WHO WILL GUIDE MY PEOPLE ISRAEL.' '' $\Big\}$ (13)

So Herod **called** the visitors . . . (24)
and found out the **exact** time the **star** had appeared. (15, 6)
Then he sent them to *Bethlehem: (*S)
''Go and . . . **search** for the **child**, (21, 3)
and when you find him **let me know**, (30)
so that I may go and **worship** him too.'' (27)

43

On their way they saw the **star** . . . (6)
and it **went ahead** of them (26)
until it stopped over the **place** where the child was. . . . (17)

They **went** into the house (26)
and saw the **child** with his mother Mary. (3)
They knelt down and **worshiped** him, (9)
and **offered him presents: gold, frankincense, and myrrh.** (11)

God warned them in a **dream** (20)
not to go back to **Herod**, (4)
so they **went back** by another road. (26)

Matt. 2, 1-12

UNIT 7—THE WISE MEN

Section B—Art Form

PROCEDURE:
Set the Scene:
—Encourage a creative picture or series of pictures.
—Review the setting. Recall the different scenes of the story by asking what people were there, what the scene looked like, expressions, moods, etc.
—Show a picture from a children's Bible, or
—Put the scene on an overhead transparency or chalk the scene on the board.

Create the Mood:
—As the materials are being passed out have slow, instrumental music playing in the background. (If music was used for "Telling the Story" use the same composition during the art.)
  At the same time it might be helpful to have one or two children reread the Gospel text.
—Remind them to share their ideas with others.

Materials:
—Ask the children to take out whatever materials are needed—crayons, felt markers, water colors etc.
—Pass out the paper.

Appreciation:
—Walk around to look at the work—encourage, offer help if needed, etc.
—Admire their finished product (sometimes hold it up, or let the child walk around and show it).

Folder:
  If possible have the children keep a Gospel folder for their pictures, plays, etc. Let them take the pictures home to show, if they wish, but encourage their return, as they will be useful during the Reflection.

ALTERNATIVES:
—Group work—give out large paper (brown roll paper, primary drawing paper, or smaller pieces taped together) and let groups of children work on different scenes.
—Make a banner (cloth or paper) for classroom or Eucharistic Celebration, or small ones for their rooms at home.
—Make puppet characters that can be used with play script. Some might work on scenery for the puppet play.
—Opaque projector work, reproducing Gospel scene with felt markers.
—Cut out stand-up figures in a 3-D scene.
—Symbol art, etc.
—Offer a ditto copy of a picture for those who wish to color it or use it as a model in drawing their own picture.

UNIT 7—THE WISE MEN

Section C—The Play

Characters: Narrator 2, Wise Man 1, 2, 3, Herod, Chief Priest, Teacher of the Law, Narrator 1. (Tableau scene—Mary and the Child.)

Narrator 1: The name of our play is:
THE WISE MEN
(Introduction of characters)

Narrator 2: Jesus was born in the town of Bethlehem. . . . Soon afterward some men who studied the stars came from the east to Jerusalem. (Matt. 2, 1)

Wise Man 1: Where is the baby born to be the king of the Jews?

Wise Man 2: We saw his star when it came up in the east.

Wise Man 3: And we have come to worship him. (Matt. 2, 2)

Narrator 1: When King Herod heard about this he was very upset, and so was everybody else in Jerusalem. He called together all the chief priests and teachers of the Law. . . . (Matt. 2, 4)

Herod: Where will the Messiah be born? (Matt. 2, 4)

Chief P.: In the town of Bethlehem, in Judea. . . . (Matt. 2, 5)

Lawyer: This is what the prophet wrote: YOU, BETHLEHEM, IN THE LAND OF JUDAH, ARE NOT BY ANY MEANS THE LEAST AMONG THE RULERS OF JUDAH: FOR FROM YOU WILL COME A LEADER WHO WILL GUIDE MY PEOPLE ISRAEL. (Matt. 2, 6)

Narrator 2: So Herod called the visitors from the east to a secret meeting and found out from them the exact time the star appeared. Then he sent them to Bethlehem . . . (Matt. 2, 7-8)

Herod: Go and make a careful search for the child, and when you find him let me know, so that I may go and worship him too. (Matt. 2, 8)

(Wise men leave)
Wise Man 1: Look, there it is! It's the same star we saw in the east!

Wise Man 2: It seems to be moving on ahead of us, leading the way!

Wise Man 3: And now the star is standing over this place as a sign to us!

(tableau of Mary and child)
Narrators 1 and 2: They went into the house and saw the child and his mother Mary. They knelt down and worshiped him; then they opened their bags and offered him presents: gold, frankincense, and myrrh. (Matt. 2, 11)

(to audience)
Wise Men 1, 2, 3: God warned us in a dream not to go back to Herod so we are going back home by another road.

UNIT 7—THE WISE MEN

Section D—RELFECTION

Questions:

From this Gospel story we can see how Jesus was going to allow himself to be found by all nations.

1. How did the wise men know about a new king in a far-off country?

2. Why didn't Herod know about this?

3. Why was Herod upset when he heard about this new king?

4. Why was Herod so anxious for the wise men to go off and find the child?

5. Did the wise men know much about Jesus until they found him? Then what do you think they learned?

6. What makes you think the three visitors were ready to obey a message from God rather than Herod?

7. Herod and his important men of the kingdom were very near to the place where Jesus was born, yet very few were aware of his existence. How can we be very near Jesus and not aware of him?

8. Name some ways you could find him right here in the classroom, or at home.

Prayer:

Close your eyes while we talk to Jesus. He is here with us. He listens to our prayer. He wants us to be AWARE OF HIS PRESENCE. Repeat after me. (10)

> LORD JESUS,
> LIKE THE WISE MEN,
> YOUR LOVE DISCOVERS ME.
> YOU SAY, "LOVE EACH OTHER!"
> YOU SAY, "HELP YOUR NEIGHBOR!"
> YOU SAY, "WATCH THE BABY!"
> I LOOK AROUND,
> AND YOU ARE EVERYWHERE!
> THANK YOU, JESUS.
> AMEN.

UNIT 8

THE FLIGHT INTO EGYPT

UNIT 8—THE FLIGHT INTO EGYPT

Section A—Telling the Story

Background: Egypt
Archelaus

Introduction: Herod expected the visitors from the east to return with news of the Messiah. We know God warned them in a dream not to return but to go back home by another way.

Repeat after me.

After they had **left**, (26)
an **angel** of the Lord appeared in a **dream** to Joseph . . . (13, 29)
"**Get up**, take the **child** and his **mother**, (13, 3, 1)
and run away to *__Egypt__ (*W)
and stay there until I tell you to leave.   (13)
Herod will be looking for the child to kill him."

So Joseph **got up**, took the **child** and his **mother**, (11, 3, 1)
and left during the **night** for Egypt, (21)
where he stayed until **Herod** died. (4)

When Herod **realized** that the visitors . . . had tricked him, (28)
he was **furious**. (5)
He gave **orders** to kill all the boys in *__Bethlehem__ . . . (14, *S)
who were two years old and **younger**. . . . (3)

What the prophet Jeremiah had **said** came true: (23)
"A SOUND IS HEARD IN RAMAH,
THE SOUND OF BITTER CRYING AND WEEPING. ⎫
RACHEL WEEPS FOR HER CHILDREN.   ⎬ (30)
SHE WEEPS AND WILL NOT BE COMFORTED, ⎭
BECAUSE THEY ARE ALL DEAD."

After Herod had **died**, (27)
an angel . . . **appeared** in a dream to Joseph and said: (17)
"Get up, take the child and his mother,
and go back to the country of Israel. . . .   } (13)
Those who tried to kill the child are dead."

So Joseph got up, **took the child and his mother**, (7)
and **went back** to the country of *Israel. (26, *N)

When he heard that **Archelaus** (2)
had succeeded his father Herod as **king** of Judea, (4)
Joseph was **afraid** to settle there. (19)
He was given more instructions in a **dream**, (29)
and so **went** to the province of Galilee, (26)
and made his home in *Nazareth. (*N)

Matt. 2, 14-23

UNIT 8—THE FLIGHT INTO EGYPT

Section B—Art Form

PROCEDURE:
Set the Scene:
—Encourage a creative picture or series of pictures.
—Review the setting. Recall the different scenes of the story by asking what people were there, what the scene looked like, expressions, moods, etc.
—Show a picture from a children's Bible, or
—Put the scene on an overhead transparency or chalk the scene on the board.

Create the Mood:
—As the materials are being passed out have slow, instrumental music playing in the background. (If music was used for "Telling the Story" use the same composition during the art.)
    At the same time it might be helpful to have one or two children reread the Gospel text.
—Remind them to share their ideas with others.

Materials:
—Ask the children to take out whatever materials are needed—crayons, felt markers, water colors etc.
—Pass out the paper.

Appreciation:
—Walk around to look at the work—encourage, offer help if needed, etc.
—Admire their finished product (sometimes hold it up, or let the child walk around and show it).

Folder:
    If possible have the children keep a Gospel folder for their pictures, plays, etc. Let them take the pictures home to show, if they wish, but encourage their return, as they will be useful during the Reflection.

ALTERNATIVES:
—Group work—give out large paper (brown roll paper, primary drawing paper, or smaller pieces taped together) and let groups of children work on different scenes.
—Make a banner (cloth or paper) for classroom or Eucharistic Celebration, or small ones for their rooms at home.
—Make puppet characters that can be used with play script. Some might work on scenery for the puppet play.
—Opaque projector work, reproducing Gospel scene with felt markers.
—Cut out stand-up figures in a 3-D scene.
—Symbol art, etc.
—Offer a ditto copy of a picture for those who wish to color it or use it as a model in drawing their own picture.

UNIT 8—THE FLIGHT INTO EGYPT

Section C—The Play

Characters: Narrator 2, Angel, Joseph, Herod, Mary and Child

Narrator 1:   The title of our play is
THE FLIGHT INTO EGYPT
(Introduction of characters)

Narrator 2:   After the wise men left to return to their own country, an angel of the Lord appeared to Joseph in a dream.

Angel: Get up, take the child and his mother, and run away to Egypt, and stay there until I tell you to leave. Herod will be looking for the child to kill him.
(Matt. 2, 13)

Joseph: Get up, Mary, and bring the child. We must leave this very night for Egypt. Herod will be looking for Jesus to kill him.

Narrator 1:   When Herod realized that the visitors from the east had tricked him, he was furious.
(Matt. 2, 16)

Herod: Soldiers! Go to Bethlehem and to all the neighborhood around and kill every baby boy two years old and younger.

Narrators 1 and 2:   What the prophet Jeremiah had said came true: "A SOUND IS HEARD IN RAMAH. . . . RACHEL WEEPS FOR HER CHILDREN . . . BECAUSE THEY ARE ALL DEAD."
(Matt. 2, 17-18)

Narrator 2:   After Herod had died, an angel of the Lord appeared in a dream to Joseph, in Egypt.
(Matt. 2, 19)

Angel: Get up, take the child and his mother, and go back to the country of Israel, because those who tried to kill the child are dead.
(Matt. 2, 20)

Joseph: Mary, the Lord has sent us word that we can go back to Israel. Herod is dead!

Narrator 1:   When he heard that Archelaus had succeeded his father Herod as king of Judea, Joseph was afraid to settle there.
(Matt. 2, 22)

Angel: You are right, Joseph, go beyond Judea to Galilee.

Narrator 2:   He . . . went to the province of Galilee and made his home in a town named Nazareth. He did this to make come true what the prophets had said, "He will be called a Nazarene."
(Matt. 2, 23)

UNIT 8—THE FLIGHT INTO EGYPT

Section D—REFLECTION

Questions:

Mary and Joseph were not aware of Herod's plot. There were no modern communications. God was aware for them and made all the necessary arrangements. Think about this story!

1. How did Joseph know Jesus was in danger?
2. What kind of preparation could Mary and Joseph have made?
3. What kind of transportation could they have had?
4. Although they knew God was always with them, do you think they had to depend on others in Egypt? In what ways?
5. How do you think they felt about the sad news from Bethlehem?
6. How was Joseph directed back to Nazareth?
7. Joseph had to depend on God to direct the little family every step of the way. How is God directing you at this stage of your life?
8. Is it easy to be dependent on others (to be sick, old, retarded, poor, etc.)?
9. Do others depend on you? How can you help them?

Prayer:

Close your eyes while we talk to Jesus. He is here with us. He listens to our prayer. He wants to HELP us. Repeat after me. (16)

> LORD JESUS,
> GUIDE ME BY YOUR HOLY SPIRIT.
> I DEPEND ON YOU.
> LET ME BE AWARE OF OTHERS,
> ESPECIALLY WHEN THEY NEED HELP.
> BE WITH ME ALWAYS, LORD JESUS.
> AMEN.

UNIT 9

THE BOY JESUS IN THE TEMPLE

UNIT 9—THE BOY JESUS IN THE TEMPLE

Section A—Telling the Story

Background: Feast of Passover

Introduction: When a Jewish boy was twelve he was old enough to attend all the feasts and celebrations required by the Law.

Repeat after me.

Every year Jesus' parents went to *Jerusalem (*S)
for the feast of **Passover**. (26)
When Jesus was twelve years old, they went to the **feast** as usual. (9)

When the days of the feast were **over**, (19)
they **started** back home, (15)
but the **boy Jesus** stayed in Jerusalem. (2)

His **parents** did not know this. (15)
They **thought** he was with the group, so they **traveled** a whole day, (20, 26)
and then started **looking** for him among . . . **relatives and friends**. (21, 7)
They did not **find** him, (29)
so they went back to *Jerusalem looking for him. (*S)

On the third day they **found** him in the temple. (9)
sitting with the Jewish **teachers**, (11, 2)
listening to them and **asking** questions. (22, 23)
All who heard him were **amazed** at his intelligent answers. (17)

His **parents** were amazed when they saw him (20)
His **mother** said to him: (1)
"Son, why did you do this to us?
Your father and I have been terribly worried trying to find you." } (16)

He **answered** them, (19)
"Why did you have to look for me?
Didn't you know that I had to be in my Father's house?" } (10)

But they did not **understand** what he said to them. (20)
So Jesus went back with them to *Nazareth, (*N)
where he was **obedient** to them. (19)

His mother **treasured** all these things in **her heart**. (9, 1)
And **Jesus** grew up, both in body and in **wisdom**, (10, 11)
gaining favor **with God and men**. (6)

Luke 2, 41-52

UNIT 9—THE BOY JESUS IN THE TEMPLE

Section B—Art Form

PROCEDURE:
Set the Scene:
—Encourage a creative picture or series of pictures.
—Review the setting. Recall the different scenes of the story by asking what people were there, what the scene looked like, expressions, moods, etc.
—Show a picture from a children's Bible, or
—Put the scene on an overhead transparency or chalk the scene on the board.

Create the Mood:
—As the materials are being passed out have slow, instrumental music playing in the background. (If music was used for "Telling the Story" use the same composition during the art.)
  At the same time it might be helpful to have one or two children reread the Gospel text.
—Remind them to share their ideas with others.

Materials:
—Ask the children to take out whatever materials are needed—crayons, felt markers, water colors etc.
—Pass out the paper.

Appreciation:
—Walk around to look at the work—encourage, offer help if needed, etc.
—Admire their finished product (sometimes hold it up, or let the child walk around and show it).

Folder:
  If possible have the children keep a Gospel folder for their pictures, plays, etc. Let them take the pictures home to show, if they wish, but encourage their return, as they will be useful during the Reflection.

ALTERNATIVES:
—Group work—give out large paper (brown roll paper, primary drawing paper, or smaller pieces taped together) and let groups of children work on different scenes.
—Make a banner (cloth or paper) for classroom or Eucharistic Celebration, or small ones for their rooms at home.
—Make puppet characters that can be used with play script. Some might work on scenery for the puppet play.
—Opaque projector work, reproducing Gospel scene with felt markers.
—Cut out stand-up figures in a 3-D scene.
—Symbol art, etc.
—Offer a ditto copy of a picture for those who wish to color it or use it as a model in drawing their own picture.

UNIT 9—THE BOY JESUS IN THE TEMPLE

Section C—The Play

Characters: Narrator 2, Mary, Joseph, Jesus, Narrator 1

Narrator 1:   The title of our play is:
THE BOY JESUS IN THE TEMPLE
(Introduction of characters)

Narrator 2:   Every year Jesus' parents went to Jerusalem for the feast of Passover. When Jesus was twelve years old, they went to the feast as usual. (Luke 2, 41-42)

Narrator 1:   When the days of the feast were over, they started back home, but the boy Jesus stayed in Jerusalem.   (Luke 2, 43)

Narrator 2:   His parents did not know this; they thought that he was with the group, so they traveled a whole day, and then started looking for him among their relatives and friends.   (Luke 2, 43-44)

Mary: Where is Jesus? I thought he was traveling with friends or relatives in our group.

Joseph: Let's ask around. (They go from group to group looking for Jesus and asking when he had last been seen. Then turning to Mary:) We must go back to Jerusalem. He must be lost!

Narrator 1:   Mary and Joseph traveled the long road back to the big city. They searched everywhere in Jerusalem, asking if anyone had seen the child.

Narrator 2:   On the third day they found him in the temple, sitting with the Jewish teachers, listening to them and asking them questions. All who heard him were amazed at his intelligent answers. His parents were amazed when they saw him.   (Luke 2, 46-48)

Mary: Son, why did you do this to us? Your father and I have been terribly worried trying to find you.   (Luke 2, 48)

Jesus: Why did you have to look for me? Didn't you know that I had to be in my Father's house?   (Luke 2, 49)

Narrator 1:   But they did not understand what he said to them. So Jesus went back with them to Nazareth, where he was obedient to them.   (Luke 2, 50-51)

Narrator 2:   His mother treasured all these things in her heart. And Jesus grew up, both in body and in wisdom, gaining favor with God and men.   (Luke 2, 51-52)

UNIT 9—THE BOY JESUS IN THE TEMPLE

Section D—REFLECTION

Questions:

By the time Jesus was twelve years old he must have known all about the feasts and services required by the Law of Moses. He was ready to ask questions about them.

1. Where did Jesus go with his parents when he was twelve years old?

2. What happened after the feast was over?

3. Why do you think Mary and Joseph didn't look in the temple right away?

4. What was Jesus doing when they found him in the temple?

5. Do you think Jesus meant to worry Mary and Joseph? How do you think he felt about what they had been through?

6. What does St. Luke tell us he did to make up to his parents and show them how much he loved and respected them?

7. When someone really doesn't understand why you want to do something, is it hard to be patient? Give an example.

8. Have you ever tried to put yourself in the place of others and try to feel the way they feel?

Prayer:

Close your eyes while we talk to Jesus. He is here with us. He listens to our prayer. He is ready to FORGIVE. Repeat after me. (16)

> LORD JESUS,
> FORGIVE ME FOR BEING CROSS.
> LORD JESUS,
> FORGIVE ME FOR BEING STUBBORN.
> LORD JESUS,
> FORGIVE ME FOR BEING MEAN.
> LORD JESUS,
> FORGIVE ME FOR BEING SELFISH.
> GIVE ME YOUR PEACE AND YOUR LOVE.
> THANK YOU, LORD JESUS.
> AMEN.

UNIT 10

THE BAPTISM OF JESUS

UNIT 10—THE BAPTISM OF JESUS

Section A—Telling the Story

Introduction: John, the son of Zechariah and Elizabeth, had gone out to the desert to pray and prepare himself for his teaching mission. Then the time came for him to help others to make themselves ready for the coming of Jesus.

Repeat after me.

John the Baptist started **preaching** in the desert of Judea. (7)
"Turn away from your sins," he said,　⎫
"for the kingdom of heaven is near!" . . . ⎰ (8)

People **came** to him from Jerusalem (26)
and from all the country **around** the Jordan river. (21)
They **confessed** their sins, and he **baptized** them in the Jordan. . . . (30, 11)

He said, "I **baptize** you with **water** (20, 16)
to show that you have **repented**; (30)
but the one who will come **after** me (15)
will **baptize** you with the **Holy Spirit** and **fire**. (11, 12, 8)
He is much greater than I am; (10)
I am **not good enough** even to carry his sandals." . . . (30)

At that time **Jesus** went from Galilee to the *Jordan, (10, *E)
and **came** to John to be baptized by him. (18)
But John **tried** to make him change his mind. (28)
"I ought to be **baptized** by you," John said, (15, 11)
"yet **you** come to **me**!" (15, 15)

Jesus answered . . . "Let it be this way for now,　⎫
for in this way we shall do all that God requires." ⎰ (17)
So John **agreed**. (19)

As soon as **Jesus** was baptized, he **came out** of the water. (10, 26)
Then heaven was **opened** to him. . . . (6)
He saw the **Spirit of God** coming **down** like a dove. . . . (8, 9)

Then a **voice** said from heaven, (22)
"**This is my own dear Son, with whom I am well pleased**." (12)

Matt. 3, 1-2, 5-6, 11, 13-17

UNIT 10—THE BAPTISM OF JESUS

Section B—Art Form

PROCEDURE:

Set the Scene:
—Encourage a creative picture or series of pictures.
—Review the setting. Recall the different scenes of the story by asking what people were there, what the scene looked like, expressions, moods, etc.
—Show a picture from a children's Bible, or
—Put the scene on an overhead transparency or chalk the scene on the board.

Create the Mood:
—As the materials are being passed out have slow, instrumental music playing in the background. (If music was used for "Telling the Story" use the same composition during the art.)
   At the same time it might be helpful to have one or two children reread the Gospel text.
—Remind them to share their ideas with others.

Materials:
—Ask the children to take out whatever materials are needed—crayons, felt markers, water colors etc.
—Pass out the paper.

Appreciation:
—Walk around to look at the work—encourage, offer help if needed, etc.
—Admire their finished product (sometimes hold it up, or let the child walk around and show it).

Folder:
   If possible have the children keep a Gospel folder for their pictures, plays, etc. Let them take the pictures home to show, if they wish, but encourage their return, as they will be useful during the Reflection.

ALTERNATIVES:
—Group work—give out large paper (brown roll paper, primary drawing paper, or smaller pieces taped together) and let groups of children work on different scenes.
—Make a banner (cloth or paper) for classroom or Eucharistic Celebration, or small ones for their rooms at home.
—Make puppet characters that can be used with play script. Some might work on scenery for the puppet play.
—Opaque projector work, reproducing Gospel scene with felt markers.
—Cut out stand-up figures in a 3-D scene.
—Symbol art, etc.
—Offer a ditto copy of a picture for those who wish to color it or use it as a model in drawing their own picture.

UNIT 10—THE BAPTISM OF JESUS

Section C—The Play

Characters: Narrator 2, John, Jesus, Narrator 1

Narrator 1:   The title of our play is:
   THE BAPTISM OF JESUS
   (Introduction of characters)

Narrator 2:   At that time John the Baptist came and started preaching in the desert of
   Judea.   (Matt. 3, 1)

John: Turn away from your sins . . . for the kingdom of heaven is near. (Matt. 3, 2)

Narrator 1:   John was the one that the prophet Isaiah was talking about when he said:
                                                               (Matt. 3, 3)

Narrators
1 and 2:   SOMEONE IS SHOUTING IN THE DESERT: GET THE LORD'S ROAD READY
   FOR HIM. MAKE A STRAIGHT PATH FOR HIM TO TRAVEL.   (Matt. 3, 3)

Narrator 2:   John's clothes were made of camel's hair; he wore a leather belt around his
   waist, and ate locusts and wild honey. People came to him from Jerusalem,
   from the whole province of Judea. . . . They confessed their sins and he
   baptized them in the Jordan.   (Matt. 3, 4-6)

John: I baptize you with water to show that you have repented; but the one who
   will come after me will baptize you with the Holy Spirit and fire. He is much
   greater than I am; I am not good enough even to carry his sandals.
                                                               (Matt. 3, 11)

Narrator 1:   At that time Jesus went from Galilee to the Jordan, and came to John to be
   baptized by him.   (Matt. 3, 13)

John: I ought to be baptized by you . . . yet you come to me!   (Matt. 3, 14)

Jesus: Let it be this way for now. For in this way we shall do all that God requires.
                                                               (Matt. 3, 15)

Narrator 2:   John agreed. As soon as Jesus was baptized, he came up out of the water.
   Then heaven was opened to him, and he saw the Spirit of God coming down
   like a dove and lighting on him. And then a voice said from heaven:
                                                               (Matt. 3, 15-17)

Narrators
1 and 2:   THIS IS MY OWN DEAR SON, WITH WHOM I AM WELL PLEASED.
                                                               (Matt. 3, 17)

UNIT 10—THE BAPTISM OF JESUS

Section D—REFLECTION

Questions:

When Jesus first started his work for the kingdom, he asked for the baptism of John. Jesus wanted the approval of the Father on his mission. The kingdom was near.

1. What was John's message in the desert?

2. How did John compare himself with Jesus?

3. Why didn't Jesus need John's baptism?

4. How did the Father show his approval of Jesus?

5. John had helped prepare the way for Jesus. Whom else had Jesus counted on to help him prepare for his work?

6. Do we count on others to help us grow so that we can do the things God asks of us? Who are they? How do they help us?

7. When you have done something well, how do you feel when others show they approve?

8. How do you show gratitude for the things others do well for you (gratitude to parents, brothers, sisters, friends, God)?

Prayer:

Close your eyes while we talk to Jesus. He is here with us. He listens to our prayer. He wants to say "YES" to us. Repeat after me. (16)

>LORD JESUS,
>I AM YOURS.
>YOU SAY "YES" TO MY LIFE,
>"YES" TO MY GIFTS,
>"YES" TO MY TALENTS,
>"YES" TO MY FAMILY.
>I LIKE ME BECAUSE
>YOU LOVE ME.
>YOU CARE ABOUT ME.
>YOU SURROUND ME WITH YOUR LIFE.
>THANK YOU, LORD JESUS.
>AMEN.

UNIT 11

THE CALL

UNIT 11—THE CALL

Section A—Telling the Story

Background: Lake Gennesaret

Introduction: Jesus had been in Judea and Galilee giving his message to all who would listen. He had visited Simon Peter's house and cured his mother-in-law of a fever. Many people gathered wherever he spoke, since he healed the sick. Here is the message he had for Peter and the apostles.

Repeat after me.

Jesus was standing on the shore of Lake Gennesaret. . . . (10)
The people **pushed** their way up to him (26)
to **listen** to the word of God. (22)

He saw two boats pulled up on the beach; (19)
the fishermen had left them and **gone off** to wash the nets. (15)

Jesus **got into** one of the boats—**it belonged to Simon**— (26, 24)
and asked him to **push off** a little from the shore. (15)
Jesus sat in the boat and **taught** the crowd. (7)

When he finished speaking he **said** to Simon, (23)
"Push the boat **out further** to the deep water (15)
and . . . **let your nets** down for a catch." (27)

"Master," Simon answered, (28)
"we worked hard **all night** . . . and caught nothing. (20)
But if **you say so**, I will let down the nets." (28)

They let the **nets down** (27)
and caught such a **large** number of fish (7)
that the nets were **about to break**. . . . (17)

They **motioned** to their partners in the other boat to . . . help. (6)
They . . . filled both boats so **full** of fish (12)
that they were about to **sink**. (27)

Simon Peter . . . **fell on his knees** before Jesus and said, (29)
"**Go away from me, Lord, for I am a sinful man!**" (18)
All . . . were **amazed** at the large number of fish. . . . (20)

Jesus said to Simon, "Don't be afraid; } (10)
from now on you will be catching men." }

They **pulled** the boats on the beach, (27)
left everything, and **followed** Jesus. (8)

Luke 5, 1-11

UNIT 11—THE CALL

Section B—Art Form

PROCEDURE:

Set the Scene:
—Encourage a creative picture or series of pictures.
—Review the setting. Recall the different scenes of the story by asking what people were there, what the scene looked like, expressions, moods, etc.
—Show a picture from a children's Bible, or
—Put the scene on an overhead transparency or chalk the scene on the board.

Create the Mood:
—As the materials are being passed out have slow, instrumental music playing in the background. (If music was used for "Telling the Story" use the same composition during the art.)
  At the same time it might be helpful to have one or two children reread the Gospel text.
—Remind them to share their ideas with others.

Materials:
—Ask the children to take out whatever materials are needed—crayons, felt markers, water colors etc.
—Pass out the paper.

Appreciation:
—Walk around to look at the work—encourage, offer help if needed, etc.
—Admire their finished product (sometimes hold it up, or let the child walk around and show it).

Folder:
  If possible have the children keep a Gospel folder for their pictures, plays, etc. Let them take the pictures home to show, if they wish, but encourage their return, as they will be useful during the Reflection.

ALTERNATIVES:
—Group work—give out large paper (brown roll paper, primary drawing paper, or smaller pieces taped together) and let groups of children work on different scenes.
—Make a banner (cloth or paper) for classroom or Eucharistic Celebration, or small ones for their rooms at home.
—Make puppet characters that can be used with play script. Some might work on scenery for the puppet play.
—Opaque projector work, reproducing Gospel scene with felt markers.
—Cut out stand-up figures in a 3-D scene.
—Symbol art, etc.
—Offer a ditto copy of a picture for those who wish to color it or use it as a model in drawing their own picture.

UNIT 11—THE CALL

Section C—The Play

Characters: Narrator 2, Jesus, Peter, James, John, Narrator 1

Narrator 1: The name of our play is:
THE CALL
(Introduction of characters)

Narrator 2: One time Jesus was standing on the shore of Lake Gennesaret while the people pushed their way up to him to listen to the word of God. He saw two boats pulled up on the beach; the fishermen had left them and gone off to wash the nets. (Luke 5, 1-2)

Narrator 1: Jesus got into one of the boats—it belonged to Simon—and asked him to push off a little from the shore. Jesus sat in the boat and taught the crowd. When he finished speaking . . . (Luke 5, 3-4)

Jesus: Push the boat out further to the deep water, and you and your partners let your nets down for a catch. (Luke 5, 4)

Peter: Master . . . we worked hard all night long and caught nothing. But if you say so, I will let down the nets. (Luke 5, 5)

Narrator 2: They let the nets down and caught such a large number of fish that the nets were about to break. So they motioned to their partners in the other boat. (Luke 5, 6-7)

Peter: Come, help us! Our boat is full and about to go down!

Narrator 1: They came and filled both boats so full of fish that they were about to sink. When Simon Peter saw what had happened he fell on his knees before Jesus. . . . (Luke 5, 7-8)

Peter: Go away from me, Lord, for I am a sinful man. (Luke 5, 8)

Narrator 2: He and all the others with him were amazed at the large number of fish! (Luke 5, 9)

James: We have never caught such a load before! What would our father, Zebedee, say about this?

John: Who is this great man who has such power over men and over the sea? We must listen to all that he says. Now he is speaking to Simon Peter!

Jesus: Don't be afraid; from now on you will be catching men. (Luke 5, 10)

Narrators 1 and 2: They pulled the boats on the beach, left everything and followed Jesus. (Luke 5, 11)

UNIT 11—THE CALL

Section D—REFLECTION

Questions:

The sea was a special place for Simon Peter and his friends. They worked there daily and knew their job well. In the story Jesus meets them while they are "on the job" and shows them his power.

1. Where were Peter and his companions when Jesus was talking to the people on the shore?
2. What do you think they could have known about Jesus?
3. What did Jesus tell them to do?
4. Do you think Peter thought Jesus was a fisherman? Explain.
5. When did Peter start thinking about who Jesus really was?
6. When Jesus saw Peter and his companions were ready to follow him, what did he say?
7. What was the message they would learn from Jesus over the next three years?
8. Does Jesus want us to carry on this message? How?

Prayer:

Close your eyes while we talk to Jesus. He is here with us. He listens to our prayer. He wants to tell us his MESSAGE. Repeat after me. (16)

> LORD JESUS,
> YOUR MESSAGE IS YOU.
> YOU LIVE YOUR MESSAGE.
> YOU SHOW GOODNESS.
> YOU ARE TRUTH.
> YOU GIVE LOVE.
> YOU FORGIVE AND BRING PEACE.
> THANK YOU, LORD JESUS.
> AMEN.

UNIT 12

THE MARRIAGE FEAST
AT CANA

UNIT 12—THE MARRIAGE FEAST AT CANA

Section A—Telling the Story

Background: Water jars

Introduction: A few days after Jesus had chosen some of his first disciples, they went to a wedding celebration. Let's see who else was there.

Repeat after me.

There was a **wedding** in the town of *Cana, in Galilee. (12, *N)
Jesus' **mother** was there. (1)
Jesus and his disciples had also been invited. . . . (7)

When all the wine **had been drunk**, (16)
Jesus' mother **said** to him, (19)
"They have no **wine**." (16)
Jesus replied . . . "**My time has not yet come**." (10)

Jesus' **mother** told the servants, (1)
"**Do whatever he tells you**." . . . (23)

Six stone **water jars** were there, (15)
each . . . to **hold** between twenty and thirty gallons. (12)
Jesus **said** to the servants, (23)
"**Fill these jars** with water." (11)

They filled them to the **brim**. . . . (7)
He told them, "Now **draw** some water out (11)
and **take it** to the **man in charge** of the feast." (16, 2)

They took it to him and he **tasted** the water, (23)
which had turned into wine. (17)

73

He **did not know where** this wine had come from (28)
(but the servant who had drawn out the water knew). (24)

So he **called** the bridegroom and said to him, (15)
"**Everyone else** serves the best wine first, (7)
and after the **guests have drunk** a lot (28)
he **serves** the ordinary wine. (16)
But you **have kept** the best wine **until** now!" (17, 28)

Jesus performed this first of his mighty works in Cana of Galilee; ⎱ (12)
there he revealed his glory, ⎰
and his disciples **believed** in him. (17)

John 2, 1-11

UNIT 12—THE MARRIAGE FEAST OF CANA

Section B—Art Form

PROCEDURE:
Set the Scene:
—Encourage a creative picture or series of pictures.
—Review the setting. Recall the different scenes of the story by asking what people were there, what the scene looked like, expressions, moods, etc.
—Show a picture from a children's Bible, or
—Put the scene on an overhead transparency or chalk the scene on the board.

Create the Mood:
—As the materials are being passed out have slow, instrumental music playing in the background. (If music was used for "Telling the Story" use the same composition during the art.)
  At the same time it might be helpful to have one or two children reread the Gospel text.
—Remind them to share their ideas with others.

Materials:
—Ask the children to take out whatever materials are needed—crayons, felt markers, water colors etc.
—Pass out the paper.

Appreciation:
—Walk around to look at the work—encourage, offer help if needed, etc.
—Admire their finished product (sometimes hold it up, or let the child walk around and show it).

Folder:
  If possible have the children keep a Gospel folder for their pictures, plays, etc. Let them take the pictures home to show, if they wish, but encourage their return, as they will be useful during the Reflection.

ALTERNATIVES:
—Group work—give out large paper (brown roll paper, primary drawing paper, or smaller pieces taped together) and let groups of children work on different scenes.
—Make a banner (cloth or paper) for classroom or Eucharistic Celebration, or small ones for their rooms at home.
—Make puppet characters that can be used with play script. Some might work on scenery for the puppet play.
—Opaque projector work, reproducing Gospel scene with felt markers.
—Cut out stand-up figures in a 3-D scene.
—Symbol art, etc.
—Offer a ditto copy of a picture for those who wish to color it or use it as a model in drawing their own picture.

UNIT 12—THE MARRIAGE FEAST AT CANA

Section C—The Play

Characters: Narrator 2, Mary, Jesus, Servant, Steward, Narrator 1, Bridegroom

Narrator 1:   The title of our play is:
THE MARRIAGE FEAST AT CANA
(Introduction of characters)

Narrator 2:   Two days later there was a wedding in the town of Cana, in Galilee. Jesus' mother was there, and Jesus and his disciples had also been invited to the wedding.   (John 2, 1-2)

Narrator 1:   Not long after the celebration started the wine ran out.

Mary: (Mary turns to Jesus)
They are out of wine!   (John 2, 3)

Jesus: You must not tell me what to do. . . . My time has not yet come.   (John 2, 4)

Mary: (Mary goes over to the servant)
Do whatever he tells you.   (John 2, 5)

Narrator 2:   The Jews have religious rules about washing, and for this purpose six stone water jars were there, each one large enough to hold between twenty and thirty gallons.   (John 2, 6)

Jesus: (Jesus to the servants)
Fill these jars with water.   (John 2, 7)

Servant: Sir, we have filled them to the brim. Now what should we do?

Jesus: Now draw some water out and take it to the man in charge of the feast.   (John 2, 8)

Narrator 1:   They took it to him, and he tasted the water, which had turned into wine. He did not know where this wine had come from (but the servants who had drawn out the water knew).   (John 2, 8-9)

Steward: (Steward of the feast to the bridegroom)
Everyone else serves the best wine first, and after the guests have drunk a lot he serves the ordinary wine. But you have kept the best wine until now!   (John 2, 10)

Narrators 1 and 2:   Jesus performed this first of his mighty works in Cana of Galilee; there he revealed his glory, and his disciples believed in him.   (John 2, 11)

Narrator 2:   After this, Jesus and his mother, brothers, and disciples went to Capernaum and stayed there a few days.   (John 2, 12)

UNIT 12—THE MARRIAGE FEAST OF CANA

Section D—REFLECTION

Questions:

Mary and Jesus were only guests at the wedding feast. But during the party they found a special way of sharing in the celebration.

1. Who came to the wedding feast?

2. When Mary saw that something was needed what did she do about it?

3. What was the reply of Jesus? And what was the reply Mary made to that answer?

4. What kind of wine did Jesus give them?

5. Was the steward happy with the "very best"?

6. Should we expect God to give us, not only what we need and ask for, but what is the "very best" for us?

7. Is it always easy to accept what is "best" for us
   • when our parents decide?
   • when the teacher says: "Do it this way"?
   • when our friends choose first?

8. How do you find out what others need? What are some ways you could give them the "very best"?

Prayer:

Close your eyes while we talk to Jesus. He is here with us. He listens to our prayer. He wants to give us the "VERY BEST." Repeat after me. (16)

> LORD JESUS,
> YOU KNOW ALL MY NEEDS.
> YOU SEE MY PROBLEMS.
> I TURN TO YOU
> AND EXPECT YOUR HELP.
> YOU TELL ME TO ASK,
> AND I KNOW YOU GIVE THE "VERY BEST."
> THANK YOU, JESUS.
> AMEN.

UNIT 13

JESUS HEALS
A PARALYZED MAN

UNIT 13—JESUS HEALS A PARALYZED MAN

Section A—Telling the Story

Background: Paralyzed
Pharisees and teachers of the Law

Introduction: After Jesus had been away for some time giving his message to the people of Judea, he came back to Capernaum. Many gathered around the house where he was staying. Even the doorway was blocked with people.

Repeat after me.

One day when **Jesus** was teaching, (10)
some **Pharisees** and **teachers of the Law** were there. . . . (2, 17)
The **power** of the Lord was present (9)
for Jesus to **heal** the sick. (12)

Some men came carrying a **paralyzed** man on a bed, (18)
and they tried to **take** him into the house (26)
and **lay** him before Jesus. (27)

Because of the **crowd** . . . (7)
they could find no way to **take** him in. (16)
So they carried him **up** on the roof, (8)
made an opening in the tiles, (27)
and **let him down** on his bed into the **middle of the group** (26, 6)
in front of **Jesus**. (10)

When Jesus saw how much **faith** they had, (9)
he **said** to the man, (23)
"**Your sins are forgiven you, my friend**." (12)

The **teachers of the Law** and the **Pharisees** (17, 2)
began to **say to themselves**: (20)
"**Who is this man** who speaks against God in this way? (28)
No **man** can **forgive sins**; (2, 12, 30)
God alone can!" (8)

Jesus **knew** their thoughts and said to them: (20)
"**Why** do you think such things? (16)
Is it easier to **say**, 'Your **sins are forgiven** you,' (23, 12)
or to **say**, '**Get up** and walk'? (23, 11)
I will **prove** to you, then, (15)
that the **Son of Man** has **authority** on **earth** to **forgive sins**." (10, 8, 10, 12)

So he said to the **paralyzed man**, (18)
"I tell you, **get up**, **pick up your bed**, and **go home**!" (11, 26, 15)

At once the man **got up**, **took** the bed he had been lying on, (16, 26)
and went home, **praising God**. (9)
They were all completely **amazed**! (20)
Full of fear, they **praised God**, saying, (8)
"What **marvelous things** we have seen today!" (17)

Luke 5, 17-26

UNIT 13—JESUS HEALS A PARALYZED MAN

Section B—Art Form

PROCEDURE:

Set the Scene:
—Encourage a creative picture or series of pictures.
—Review the setting. Recall the different scenes of the story by asking what people were there, what the scene looked like, expressions, moods, etc.
—Show a picture from a children's Bible, or
—Put the scene on an overhead transparency or chalk the scene on the board.

Create the Mood:
—As the materials are being passed out have slow, instrumental music playing in the background. (If music was used for "Telling the Story" use the same composition during the art.)
  At the same time it might be helpful to have one or two children reread the Gospel text.
—Remind them to share their ideas with others.

Materials:
—Ask the children to take out whatever materials are needed—crayons, felt markers, water colors etc.
—Pass out the paper.

Appreciation:
—Walk around to look at the work—encourage, offer help if needed, etc.
—Admire their finished product (sometimes hold it up, or let the child walk around and show it).

Folder:
  If possible have the children keep a Gospel folder for their pictures, plays, etc. Let them take the pictures home to show, if they wish, but encourage their return, as they will be useful during the Reflection.

ALTERNATIVES:
—Group work—give out large paper (brown roll paper, primary drawing paper, or smaller pieces taped together) and let groups of children work on different scenes.
—Make a banner (cloth or paper) for classroom or Eucharistic Celebration, or small ones for their rooms at home.
—Make puppet characters that can be used with play script. Some might work on scenery for the puppet play.
—Opaque projector work, reproducing Gospel scene with felt markers.
—Cut out stand-up figures in a 3-D scene.
—Symbol art, etc.
—Offer a ditto copy of a picture for those who wish to color it or use it as a model in drawing their own picture.

UNIT 13—JESUS HEALS A PARALYZED MAN

Section C—The Play

Characters: Narrator 2, Friend 1, 2, 3, 4, Jesus, Teacher of the Law, Pharisee, paralyzed man

Narrator 1:   The title of our play is:
JESUS HEALS A PARALYZED MAN
(Introduction of characters)

Narrator 2:   One day when Jesus was teaching, some Pharisees and teachers of the Law were sitting there who had come from every town in Galilee and Judea, and from Jerusalem.   (Luke 5, 17)

Narrator 1:   The power of the Lord was present for Jesus to heal the sick. Some men came carrying a paralyzed man on a bed, and they tried to take him into the house and lay him before Jesus.   (Luke 5, 17-18)

Friend 1:   Look at the crowd around the house. They are blocking the doorway!

Friend 2:   I have an idea! We will take him to the roof by the outside stairs and see if there is an opening into the house.

(Slowly they take the paralyzed man up the steps to the roof.)
Friend 3:   You were right. There are the skylight tiles. Let's take them off!

Friend 4:   Now tie the ropes to each corner of the mat and lower him through that opening. Slow . . . easy now. There, right at the feet of Jesus!

Jesus: (Looking up at the four) What faith you have!

(Looking down at the paralyzed man) Your sins are forgiven you, my friend.
                                                      (Luke 5, 20)

Teacher of the Law: (Mumbling to themselves—turning aside from Jesus)
Who is this man who speaks against God in this way?   (Luke 5, 21)

Pharisee: No man can forgive sins! God alone can!   (Luke 5, 21)

Jesus: Why do you think such things? Is it easier to say, "Your sins are forgiven you," or to say, "Get up and walk"? I will prove to you that the Son of Man has authority on earth to forgive sins. (Pointing to the paralyzed man) I tell you, get up, pick up your bed, and go home.   (Luke 5, 22-24)

Paralyzed man: (Getting up) Look, I can move! I can stand up and even roll up my own mat! I thank you and praise God for his wonderful healing power. Praise him! Praise him!

Narrator 2:   They were all completely amazed! Full of fear, they praised God. (Luke 5, 26)

Everyone: What marvelous things we have seen today!   (Luke 5, 26)

UNIT 13—JESUS HEALS A PARALYZED MAN

Section D—REFLECTION

Questions:

In this story Jesus wanted to help everybody—the man who was paralyzed, the Pharisees, and the teachers of the law. With people working together and trying to understand, everything went well.

1. Who helped the paralyzed man get to Jesus?
2. Did the four friends give up when they arrived and found the crowd blocking the door? What happened?
3. How did Jesus use the presence of the paralyzed man to prove a point to the Pharisees?
4. Could the paralyzed man have been of some help to Jesus?
5. How do you think the four friends felt when they saw the man they had carried walk out with his bed?
6. How did that man feel toward the four friends?
7. Does God often use us to help him spread the good news of the Kingdom? How?
8. Are there times when you can't do something by yourself, and you are happy when someone comes along to help.
9. How are you like one of those four friends, trying to help out at home or at school?

Prayer:

Close your eyes while we talk to Jesus. He is here with us. He listens to our prayer. He wants to be your special FRIEND. Repeat after me. (16)

LORD JESUS,
YOU ARE MY FRIEND.
I WANT TO BE A FRIEND TO OTHERS.
MY MOTHER NEEDS A FRIEND
WHEN THERE'S TOO MUCH WORK TO DO.
MY NEIGHBOR NEEDS A FRIEND;
SHE OFTEN FEELS LEFT OUT.
THAT LITTLE BOY NEEDS A FRIEND;
HE'S LOST HIS ONLY DIME.
DO YOU WANT EVERYBODY TO BE FRIENDS?
I KNEW IT!
THANK YOU, LORD JESUS.
AMEN.

UNIT 14

JESUS CALMS A STORM

UNIT 14—JESUS CALMS A STORM

Section A—Telling the Story

Introduction: All day long Jesus had been teaching the crowd, and healing the sick. He was very tired as they crossed the lake that evening.

Repeat after me.

On the evening of that **same** day (15)
Jesus said to his disciples, (10)
"Let us go across to the **other side** of the lake." (15)

So they **left** the crowd; (26)
the disciples **got into** the boat . . . and took him with them. . . . (27)

A very **strong wind** blew up (21)
and the waves began **to spill over** into the boat (17)
so that it was about **to fill** with water. (27)

Jesus was in the **back** of the boat, (15)
sleeping with his **head** on a pillow. (20)
The disciples **woke** him up and said, (27)
"**Teacher**, don't you care that we are **about to die**?" (24, 29)

Jesus **got up** (26)
and **commanded the wind**: "Be quiet!" (13)
and **said to the waves**: "Be still!" (7)
The wind **died down**, and there was a **great calm.** (10, 19)

Then Jesus **said** to them, (23)
"**Why** are you frightened? Are you still without **faith**?" (16, 9)

But they were terribly **afraid**, (29)
and began to **say** to each other, (23)
"**Who** is this man? (28)
Even the **wind and the waves** obey him!" (6)

Mark 4, 35-41

UNIT 14—JESUS CALMS A STORM

Section B—Art Form

PROCEDURE:

Set the Scene:
—Encourage a creative picture or series of pictures.
—Review the setting. Recall the different scenes of the story by asking what people were there, what the scene looked like, expressions, moods, etc.
—Show a picture from a children's Bible, or
—Put the scene on an overhead transparency or chalk the scene on the board.

Create the Mood:
—As the materials are being passed out have slow, instrumental music playing in the background. (If music was used for "Telling the Story" use the same composition during the art.)
At the same time it might be helpful to have one or two children reread the Gospel text.
—Remind them to share their ideas with others.

Materials:
—Ask the children to take out whatever materials are needed—crayons, felt markers, water colors etc.
—Pass out the paper.

Appreciation:
—Walk around to look at the work—encourage, offer help if needed, etc.
—Admire their finished product (sometimes hold it up, or let the child walk around and show it).

Folder:
If possible have the children keep a Gospel folder for their pictures, plays, etc. Let them take the pictures home to show, if they wish, but encourage their return, as they will be useful during the Reflection.

ALTERNATIVES:
—Group work—give out large paper (brown roll paper, primary drawing paper, or smaller pieces taped together) and let groups of children work on different scenes.
—Make a banner (cloth or paper) for classroom or Eucharistic Celebration, or small ones for their rooms at home.
—Make puppet characters that can be used with play script. Some might work on scenery for the puppet play.
—Opaque projector work, reproducing Gospel scene with felt markers.
—Cut out stand-up figures in a 3-D scene.
—Symbol art, etc.
—Offer a ditto copy of a picture for those who wish to color it or use it as a model in drawing their own picture.

UNIT 14—JESUS CALMS A STORM

Section C—The Play

Characters: Jesus, Peter, James, John, Narrator

Narrator: The title of our play is:
JESUS CALMS A STORM
(Introduction of characters)
It was evening of that same day and the crowd was leaving. Jesus stood on the shore with his disciples.

Jesus: Let us go across to the other side of the lake.   (Mark 4, 35)

Narrator: The disciples got into the boat that Jesus was already in, and took him with them. A very strong wind blew up and the waves began to spill over into the boat. . . . Jesus was in the back of the boat sleeping with his head on a pillow.   (Mark 4, 36-38)

James: Look, the storm is getting worse! Are the sails well roped in?

Peter: Quickly, bail out the water. The waves are filling the boat.

John: Hurry, any more water and we will sink!

James: How can the Master sleep through this. Peter, wake him up!

Peter: Teacher, don't you care that we are about to die?   (Mark 4, 38)

Jesus: (Jesus stands up, holds up his hands to the sky)
BE QUIET!
(and turning the palms of his hands to the sea)
BE STILL!   (Mark 4, 39)

Narrator: The wind died down, and there was a great calm.   (Mark 4, 39)

Jesus: Why are you frightened? Are you still without faith?   (Mark 4, 40)

Narrator: But they were terribly afraid!   (Mark 4, 41)

John
and James: Who is this man?   (Mark 4, 41)

Peter: Even the wind and waves obey him.   (Mark 4, 41)

UNIT 14—JESUS CALMS A STORM

Section D—REFLECTION

Questions:

In this story it took a very bad storm to teach the apostles a lesson.

1. What happened after Jesus went to sleep in the boat?
2. Why did they awaken Jesus? What did they think he would do?
3. Were they thinking that Jesus might drown?
4. How did Jesus solve the problem?
5. What was an even more important fact to Jesus?
6. When we turn to God and expect him to help, what does he want of us?
7. Sometimes it takes courage to be strong. Can you think of a time when you turned to God for the courage to:
   • get a job done?
   • be kind to someone who was mean?
   • accept a disappointment?

Prayer:

Close your eyes while we talk to Jesus. He is here with us. He listens to our prayer. He tells us not to FEAR. Repeat after me. (10)

> LORD JESUS,
> YOU ARE WITH ME EVERYWHERE.
> I BELIEVE IN YOUR POWER.
> EVEN WHEN IT SEEMS YOU ARE NOT THERE,
> HELP ME TO TRUST IN YOU.
> YOU ARE THE JOY OF MY LIFE.
> HELP ME TO BE JOY FOR OTHERS.
> I LOVE YOU, JESUS.
> AMEN.

UNIT 15

JAIRUS' DAUGHTER

UNIT 15—JAIRUS' DAUGHTER

Section A—Telling the Story

Background: Synagogue
Mourning

Introduction: This story takes place in Capernaum where everyone knew Jesus and crowded around him whenever he came to town.

Repeat after me.

When Jesus **returned** to the other side of the lake (26)
the crowd **welcomed** him. (7)
They **had . . . been waiting** for him. (28)

Then a **man** named Jairus arrived, (2)
an **official** in the local synagogue. (17)
He **threw** himself down at Jesus' feet (27)
and **begged** him to go to his home. . . . (9)
His only **daughter**, twelve years old, **was dying**. (1, 29)

As **Jesus** went along, (10)
the people were **crowding** him from every side. (7)

A **messenger** came from the official's house. (17)
"**Your daughter has died**," he told Jairus; (24)
"don't **bother** the Teacher any longer." (20)
But Jesus **heard** it and said to Jairus, (22)
"Don't be afraid;
only believe, and she will be well." } (10)

When he **arrived** at the house (26)
he would not let **anyone** go in with him (15)
except Peter, John, and James,
and the child's father and mother. } (25)

Everyone . . . was **crying and mourning** for the child. (29)
Jesus **said**, "Don't cry; (23)
the child is **not dead**—she is only **sleeping!**" (29, 20)

They all **made fun** of him, (28)
because they **knew** that she was **dead**. . . . (20, 29)
Jesus **took** her by the hand and **called out**, (27, 24)
"Get up, child!" (24)

Her life returned and she **got up** at once. . . . (26)
Jesus ordered them to **give** her something to eat. (16)
Her parents were **astounded**, (17)
but Jesus **commanded** them (15)
not to tell **anything** that had happened. (10)

Luke 8, 40-42, 49-56

UNIT 15—JAIRUS' DAUGHTER

Section B—Art Form

PROCEDURE:

Set the Scene:
—Encourage a creative picture or series of pictures.
—Review the setting. Recall the different scenes of the story by asking what people were there, what the scene looked like, expressions, moods, etc.
—Show a picture from a children's Bible, or
—Put the scene on an overhead transparency or chalk the scene on the board.

Create the Mood:
—As the materials are being passed out have slow, instrumental music playing in the background. (If music was used for "Telling the Story" use the same composition during the art.)
    At the same time it might be helpful to have one or two children reread the Gospel text.
—Remind them to share their ideas with others.

Materials:
—Ask the children to take out whatever materials are needed—crayons, felt markers, water colors etc.
—Pass out the paper.

Appreciation:
—Walk around to look at the work—encourage, offer help if needed, etc.
—Admire their finished product (sometimes hold it up, or let the child walk around and show it).

Folder:
    If possible have the children keep a Gospel folder for their pictures, plays, etc. Let them take the pictures home to show, if they wish, but encourage their return, as they will be useful during the Reflection.

ALTERNATIVES:
—Group work—give out large paper (brown roll paper, primary drawing paper, or smaller pieces taped together) and let groups of children work on different scenes.
—Make a banner (cloth or paper) for classroom or Eucharistic Celebration, or small ones for their rooms at home.
—Make puppet characters that can be used with play script. Some might work on scenery for the puppet play.
—Opaque projector work, reproducing Gospel scene with felt markers.
—Cut out stand-up figures in a 3-D scene.
—Symbol art, etc.
—Offer a ditto copy of a picture for those who wish to color it or use it as a model in drawing their own picture.

UNIT 15—JAIRUS' DAUGHTER

Section C—The Play

Characters: Narrator 2, Jairus, Messenger, Jesus, Parents, Narrator 1

Narrator 1: The title of our play is:
JAIRUS' DAUGHTER
(Introduction of characters)

Narrator 2: When Jesus returned to the other side of the lake the crowd welcomed him, for they had all been waiting for him. (Luke 8, 40)

Narrator 1: Then a man named Jairus arrived, an official in the local synagogue. He threw himself down at Jesus' feet. . . . (Luke 8, 41)

Jairus: Sir, my little daughter, just twelve years old, is very sick. Please come to my house and lay your hands on her and cure her.

Narrator 2: As Jesus was going with the man to his house many people came near him, expecting to be cured. He healed them and spoke of their great faith. Before he could move along a messenger from the house of Jairus arrived.

Messenger: Your daughter has died. . . . Don't bother the Teacher any longer. (Luke 8, 49)

(Jesus also hears the messenger)
Jesus: Don't be afraid; only believe, and she will be well. (Luke 8, 50)

Narrator 1: When he arrived at the house he would not let anyone go in with him except Peter, John and James, and the child's father and mother. (Loud crying and mourning) (Luke 8, 51)

Jesus: Don't cry; the child is not dead—she is only sleeping. (loud laughing from crowd) (Luke 8, 52)

Narrator 2: They all made fun of him because they knew that she was dead. (Luke 8, 53)

Jesus: (Jesus takes the child by the hand)
GET UP, CHILD!
(The child sits up)
Now give her something to eat. (Luke 8, 54)

Parents: Praise God. Praise God and bless his holy name! How can we ever thank you, Master!

Jesus: Do not tell anyone what has happened.

UNIT 15—JAIRUS' DAUGHTER

Section D—REFLECTION

Questions:

Jesus helped everybody who believed in him whether they were important people or not. Often he would ask them to be patient and wait until he was ready to answer them.

1. Who was Jairus? What was he asking of Jesus?
2. How do you think Jairus felt when the people stopped Jesus on the way?
3. What news did the messenger bring to Jairus?
4. How did Jairus show great faith at that moment?
5. What was the immediate reward?
6. After Jesus raised the little girl, what did he say that showed everyone she was perfectly well?
7. Can you remember a time when it was hard to go on having faith because the answer was slow in coming?
8. Are there times when you try to think of the needs, sorrows, or concerns of others even though yours are important too?

Prayer:

Close your eyes while we talk to Jesus. He is here with us. He listens to our prayer. He tells us to have FAITH. Repeat after me. (16)

> LORD JESUS,
> I HAVE FAITH IN YOU.
> LET ME BE GLAD WHEN YOU HELP OTHERS.
> I KNOW THEY ARE GLAD FOR ME.
> LET ME THINK OF THEIR NEEDS BEFORE MY OWN.
> YOU ALWAYS KEEP US IN MIND.
> THANK YOU, LORD JESUS.
> AMEN.

UNIT 16

FEEDING THE FIVE THOUSAND

UNIT 16—FEEDING THE FIVE THOUSAND

Section A—Telling the Story

Introduction: Jesus had sent the disciples off to the villages and towns of Israel to preach the good news and to heal the people. This story starts with their return.

Repeat after me.

The apostles **came back** (26)
and **told** Jesus **everything** they **had done**. (17, 7, 12)
He took them . . . off by themselves to . . . Bethsaida. (26)

When the **crowds heard** about it they **followed**. . . . (7, 22, 19)
He **welcomed** them, (10)
and **spoke** to them about the **Kingdom of God**, (23, 9)
and **healed** those who needed it. (12)

When the **sun** had begun to set, (21)
the twelve disciples **came** to him and said, (19)
"Send the people away
so they can go to villages . . . around here
and find food and lodging;
for this is a lonely place." } (28)

But Jesus **said** to them, (19)
"You yourselves **give them** something to eat." (10)

They answered, "All we have is five loaves and two fish.
Do you want us to . . . buy food for this whole crowd?" } (20)
(There were about five thousand men there.) (24)

Jesus **said** to his disciples, (23)
"Make the people **sit down** in groups of about fifty each." (7)
The disciples . . . made them all **sit down**. (27)

Jesus **took** the five loaves and two fish, (16)
looked up to heaven, **thanked** God for them, (11, 8)
broke them and **gave** them to the disciples (7)
to **distribute** to the people. (27)

They all **ate** and had enough; (23)
and the disciples took up **twelve** baskets (20)
of what the people **left over**. (16)

Luke 9, 10-17

UNIT 16—FEEDING THE FIVE THOUSAND

Section B—Art Form

PROCEDURE:

Set the Scene:
—Encourage a creative picture or series of pictures.
—Review the setting. Recall the different scenes of the story by asking what people were there, what the scene looked like, expressions, moods, etc.
—Show a picture from a children's Bible, or
—Put the scene on an overhead transparency or chalk the scene on the board.

Create the Mood:
—As the materials are being passed out have slow, instrumental music playing in the background. (If music was used for "Telling the Story" use the same composition during the art.)
  At the same time it might be helpful to have one or two children reread the Gospel text.
—Remind them to share their ideas with others.

Materials:
—Ask the children to take out whatever materials are needed—crayons, felt markers, water colors etc.
—Pass out the paper.

Appreciation:
—Walk around to look at the work—encourage, offer help if needed, etc.
—Admire their finished product (sometimes hold it up, or let the child walk around and show it).

Folder:
  If possible have the children keep a Gospel folder for their pictures, plays, etc. Let them take the pictures home to show, if they wish, but encourage their return, as they will be useful during the Reflection.

ALTERNATIVES:
—Group work—give out large paper (brown roll paper, primary drawing paper, or smaller pieces taped together) and let groups of children work on different scenes.
—Make a banner (cloth or paper) for classroom or Eucharistic Celebration, or small ones for their rooms at home.
—Make puppet characters that can be used with play script. Some might work on scenery for the puppet play.
—Opaque projector work, reproducing Gospel scene with felt markers.
—Cut out stand-up figures in a 3-D scene.
—Symbol art, etc.
—Offer a ditto copy of a picture for those who wish to color it or use it as a model in drawing their own picture.

UNIT 16—FEEDING THE FIVE THOUSAND

Section C—The Play

Characters: Narrator 2, Peter, Jesus, James, John, Narrator 1

Narrator 1:   The title of our play is:
FEEDING THE FIVE THOUSAND
(Introduction of characters)

Narrator 2:   Jesus had sent the disciples out to all the villages to preach the good news and heal the people everywhere. When they came back he took them to Bethsaida to rest.

Narrator 1:   When the crowds heard about this they followed him. He welcomed them, spoke to them about the Kingdom of God, and healed those who needed it.
(Luke 9, 11)

Narrator 2:   When the sun had begun to set, the twelve came to him.   (Luke 9, 12)

Peter: Send the people away so they can go to the villages and farms around here and find food and lodging: for this is a lonely place.   (Luke 9, 12)

Jesus: You give them something to eat.   (Luke 9, 13)

James: All we have is five loaves and two fish. Do you want us to go and buy food for the whole crowd?   (Luke 9, 13)

Jesus: Make the people sit down in groups of about fifty each.   (Luke 9, 14)

Narrator 1:   The disciples . . . made them all sit down. Jesus took the five loaves and two fish, looked up to heaven, thanked God for them, broke them and gave them to the disciples.   (Luke 9, 15-16)

Jesus: Go and give this out to the people.

John: Lord, they have all eaten and had enough!

Jesus: Now pass through the crowd and gather anything that is left.

Narrator 2:   The disciples took up twelve baskets of what the people left over.
(Luke 9, 17)

UNIT 16—FEEDING THE FIVE THOUSAND

Section D—REFLECTION

Questions:

Jesus was always showing the disciples how to be generous. They were to pass on the good news about loving and caring for others. One day he taught this lesson on a hillside near the lake.

1. What had Jesus planned for the disciples when they came back from their teaching mission? What happened?

2. How do you think the disciples felt about that crowd?

3. When evening came what did the disciples say to Jesus?

4. What did Jesus do to show that he cared about the needs of the people?

5. How did the disciples share in the concern Jesus had for those men and women?

6. How can we share in the love and care Jesus has for those around us
   • on the playground?
   • in the classroom?
   • at home?

Prayer:

Close your eyes while we talk to Jesus. He is here with us. He listens to our prayer. He tells us to have CONCERN for others. Repeat after me. (10)

> LORD JESUS,
> SOMETIMES I'M TIRED
> AND I DON'T WANT TO HELP OR BE NICE.
> HELP ME AT TIMES LIKE THESE.
> LET ME SMILE AND SAY, "OH, I'D LOVE TO,"
> OR, "I WAS JUST GOING TO OFFER!"
> JESUS, YOU MUST HAVE DONE THIS TOO!
> THANK YOU, LORD.
> AMEN.

UNIT 17

MARY AND MARTHA

UNIT 17—MARY AND MARTHA

Section A—Telling the Story

Introduction: When Jesus went on his journeys he often passed through Bethany to visit his good friends Martha, Mary and Lazarus. In this story St. Luke tells us about one of those visits.

Repeat after me.

As Jesus and his disciples **went** on their way, (26)
he came to a certain **village** (17)
where a **woman** named Martha **welcomed** him to her home. (1, 10)

She had a **sister** named Mary (1)
who **sat** at the feet of the Lord (27)
and **listened** to his teaching. (20)

Martha was **upset** over all the **work** she had to do; (29, 27)
she came and said, "Lord, don't you care
that my sister has left me to do all the work by myself? } (28)
Tell her to come and help me!"

The Lord answered, "**Martha, Martha**, (16)
you are worried and **troubled** over so many things, (20)
but **just one** is needed. (15)
Mary has chosen the **right thing**, (10)
and **it** will not be taken away from her." (9)

Luke 10, 38-42

UNIT 17—MARY AND MARTHA

Section B—Art Form

PROCEDURE:

Set the Scene:
—Encourage a creative picture or series of pictures.
—Review the setting. Recall the different scenes of the story by asking what people were there, what the scene looked like, expressions, moods, etc.
—Show a picture from a children's Bible, or
—Put the scene on an overhead transparency or chalk the scene on the board.

Create the Mood:
—As the materials are being passed out have slow, instrumental music playing in the background. (If music was used for "Telling the Story" use the same composition during the art.)
At the same time it might be helpful to have one or two children reread the Gospel text.
—Remind them to share their ideas with others.

Materials:
—Ask the children to take out whatever materials are needed—crayons, felt markers, water colors etc.
—Pass out the paper.

Appreciation:
—Walk around to look at the work—encourage, offer help if needed, etc.
—Admire their finished product (sometimes hold it up, or let the child walk around and show it).

Folder:
If possible have the children keep a Gospel folder for their pictures, plays, etc. Let them take the pictures home to show, if they wish, but encourage their return, as they will be useful during the Reflection.

ALTERNATIVES:
—Group work—give out large paper (brown roll paper, primary drawing paper, or smaller pieces taped together) and let groups of children work on different scenes.
—Make a banner (cloth or paper) for classroom or Eucharistic Celebration, or small ones for their rooms at home.
—Make puppet characters that can be used with play script. Some might work on scenery for the puppet play.
—Opaque projector work, reproducing Gospel scene with felt markers.
—Cut out stand-up figures in a 3-D scene.
—Symbol art, etc.
—Offer a ditto copy of a picture for those who wish to color it or use it as a model in drawing their own picture.

UNIT 17—MARY AND MARTHA

Section C—The Play

Characters: Narrator 2, Martha, Mary, Jesus, Narrator 1

Narrator 1:   The title of our play is:
MARY AND MARTHA
(Introduction of characters)

Narrator 2:   When Jesus and his disciples went up to Jerusalem they often visited with friends on the way. Jesus liked to pass through Bethany to see Lazarus and his sisters Martha and Mary. One day Jesus arrived in Bethany.

Martha: Welcome to our home, Jesus! Come in and share a meal with us.

Mary: Master, we are so happy you came. Sit here and rest while the food is being prepared. Tell me about your teaching and the message you have come to bring.
(Mary sits down at the feet of Jesus.)

Narrator 1:   But as Martha worked at getting the meal and Mary sat and listened to Jesus, the tension grew. Martha put down her things and went to Jesus.

Martha: Lord, don't you care that my sister has left me to do all the work by myself? Tell her to come and help me.   (Luke 10, 40)

Jesus: Martha, Martha! you are worried and troubled over so many things, but just one is needed. Mary has chosen the right thing, and it will not be taken away from her.   (Luke 10, 42)

UNIT 17—MARY AND MARTHA

Section D—REFLECTION

Questions:

Martha and Mary loved Jesus, and he loved them. In this story Jesus tells us what he wants to be to us, and what we should be to others.

1. How do we know that Martha was happy to see Jesus?

2. Martha loved cooking for Jesus, so why then was she unhappy?

3. When Mary sat at the feet of Jesus listening to his message, what did she learn? Did that message include Martha? How?

4. What did Martha come in to say? What was the answer Jesus gave her?

5. What was the message about the Kingdom that Jesus had been teaching to all people: rich or poor, healthy or sick, children or adults, good or bad, Jews or foreigners, concerning love, justice, caring and sharing?

6. Later, when Martha and Mary talked together about the message they had heard from Jesus, what did they discover?

7. How do you think Martha and Mary treated each other after that visit of Jesus?

8. What do you think Jesus would say to you if you sat at his feet and listened?

Prayer:

Close your eyes while we talk to Jesus. He is here with us. He listens to our prayer. He tells us to listen for our MESSAGE. Repeat after me. (16)

> LORD JESUS,
> YOUR MESSAGE IS FOR EVERYONE:
> TO FORGIVE IF I'VE BEEN HURT,
> TO MAKE UP IF I'M AT FAULT,
> TO SHARE WHAT'S MINE TO GIVE,
> TO CARE NO MATTER WHAT!
> YOU SAID IT'S "LOVING OTHERS," LORD.
> HELP ME TO DO MY PART.
> AMEN.

UNIT 18

THE TEN LEPERS

UNIT 18—THE TEN LEPERS

Section A—Telling the Story

Background: Leper

Introduction: Lepers were not allowed to live in towns or to come near other people because of their dreadful sickness. So the ten men in this story stood off by themselves as they spoke to Jesus.

Repeat after me.

As Jesus made his way to *Jerusalem (*S)
he **went** between Samaria and Galilee. (26)

He was going into a **certain** village (15)
when he was met by ten **lepers**. (18)

They stood at a **distance** and **shouted**, (7, 24)
"**Jesus! Master! Have pity on us!**" (11)

Jesus saw them and **said** to them, (23)
"**Go** and let the priests **examine** you." (15, 16)
On the way they were **made clean**. (17)

One of them, when he **saw** that he was healed, (20)
came back, **praising God** with a loud voice. (26, 24)
He **threw** himself . . . at Jesus' feet, **thanking** him. (27, 9)
The man .vas a **Samaritan**. (17)

Jesus spoke up: (10)
"There were ten men made clean; ⎫ (28)
where are the other nine? ⎭
Why was this foreigner the only one ⎫ (16)
who came back to give thanks to God?" ⎭

And Jesus **said** to him, (23)
"**Get up and go**; (15)
your **faith** has **made you well**." (9, 12)

Luke 17, 11-19

UNIT 18—THE TEN LEPERS

Section B—Art Form

PROCEDURE:

Set the Scene:
—Encourage a creative picture or series of pictures.
—Review the setting. Recall the different scenes of the story by asking what people were there, what the scene looked like, expressions, moods, etc.
—Show a picture from a children's Bible, or
—Put the scene on an overhead transparency or chalk the scene on the board.

Create the Mood:
—As the materials are being passed out have slow, instrumental music playing in the background. (If music was used for "Telling the Story" use the same composition during the art.)
   At the same time it might be helpful to have one or two children reread the Gospel text.
—Remind them to share their ideas with others.

Materials:
—Ask the children to take out whatever materials are needed—crayons, felt markers, water colors etc.
—Pass out the paper.

Appreciation:
—Walk around to look at the work—encourage, offer help if needed, etc.
—Admire their finished product (sometimes hold it up, or let the child walk around and show it).

Folder:
   If possible have the children keep a Gospel folder for their pictures, plays, etc. Let them take the pictures home to show, if they wish, but encourage their return, as they will be useful during the Reflection.

ALTERNATIVES:

—Group work—give out large paper (brown roll paper, primary drawing paper, or smaller pieces taped together) and let groups of children work on different scenes.
—Make a banner (cloth or paper) for classroom or Eucharistic Celebration, or small ones for their rooms at home.
—Make puppet characters that can be used with play script. Some might work on scenery for the puppet play.
—Opaque projector work, reproducing Gospel scene with felt markers.
—Cut out stand-up figures in a 3-D scene.
—Symbol art, etc.
—Offer a ditto copy of a picture for those who wish to color it or use it as a model in drawing their own picture.

UNIT 18—THE TEN LEPERS

Section C—The Play

Characters: Narrator 2, Lepers, Jesus, Narrator 1

Narrator 1: The title of our play is:
THE TEN LEPERS
(Introduction of characters)

Narrator 2: As Jesus made his way to Jerusalem he went between Samaria and Galilee. He was going into a certain village when he was met by ten lepers. They stood at a distance and shouted . . .   (Luke 17, 11-13)

Lepers: Jesus! Master! Have pity on us!   (Luke 17, 13)

Jesus: Go and let the priests examine you.   (Luke 17, 14)

Narrator 1: As they turned to hobble away they realized that they had been healed. They ran and jumped and danced with joy as they went off down the road. But one stood still, remembered Jesus and turned back, praising God with a loud voice. This man was a Samaritan.

Jesus: (Samaritan throws himself at the feet of Jesus.)
There were ten men made clean; where are the other nine? Why is this foreigner the only one who came back to give thanks to God?
(Luke 17, 17-18)

Narrator 2: Jesus stretched out his hand and helped the man to his feet.

Jesus: Get up and go; your faith has made you well.   (Luke 17, 19)

107

UNIT 18—THE TEN LEPERS

Section D—REFLECTION

Questions:

This story is all about the sick people Jesus helped. It might say something to us about giving and receiving.

1. What happened when Jesus was on the road between Samaria and Galilee?

2. When were the lepers cured? Why do you think they forgot to turn back to Jesus?

3. Why was Jesus disappointed that only the Samaritan returned? Who could the others have been?

4. Do we ever "turn back" to thank our family? What often happens on Christmas and birthdays when the gift itself is so exciting?

5. Why do we sometimes show more gratitude to friends than to family?

6. Besides the big holidays, what are some everyday gifts we can give to others?

7. Do we ever stop to thank Jesus for the gifts we receive through baptism, the Eucharist, reconciliation, etc.?

Prayer:

Close your eyes while we talk to Jesus. He is here with us. He listens to our prayer. He tells us to be GRATEFUL. Repeat after me. (16)

> LORD JESUS,
> I THANK YOU FOR THE GIFT OF LIFE,
> FOR YOUR EVERYDAY GIFTS OF LOVE,
> FOR MY PARENTS AND FRIENDS,
> FOR ALL THE HELP YOU GIVE ME,
> BECAUSE I AM LITTLE AND WEAK WITHOUT YOU.
> YOU ARE MY SAVIOR.
> I NEED YOU.
> AMEN.

UNIT 19

JESUS AND THE CHILDREN

UNIT 19—JESUS AND THE CHILDREN

Section A—Telling the Story

Introduction: Everyone loves little children. It was a real treat for Jesus when he could take some time to be with them. This is the story.

Repeat after me.

Some people brought **children** to Jesus (3)
for him to **touch** them, (12)
but the disciples **scolded** those people. (15)

When Jesus **noticed** it, he was **angry** (19, 28)
and **said** to his disciples: (23)
"Let the children come to me; } (10)
do not stop them,
because the **Kingdom of God** belongs to such as **these**. (8, 10)
Remember this!
Whoever does not **receive** the **Kingdom of God** (9, 8)
like a **child** (16)
will never **enter** it." (15)

Then he **took** the children in his arms, (7)
placed his hands on each of them, (27)
and **blessed** them. (12)

Mark 10, 13-16

109

UNIT 19—JESUS AND THE CHILDREN

Section B—Art Form

PROCEDURE:

Set the Scene:
—Encourage a creative picture or series of pictures.
—Review the setting. Recall the different scenes of the story by asking what people were there, what the scene looked like, expressions, moods, etc.
—Show a picture from a children's Bible, or
—Put the scene on an overhead transparency or chalk the scene on the board.

Create the Mood:
—As the materials are being passed out have slow, instrumental music playing in the background. (If music was used for "Telling the Story" use the same composition during the art.)
   At the same time it might be helpful to have one or two children reread the Gospel text.
—Remind them to share their ideas with others.

Materials:
—Ask the children to take out whatever materials are needed—crayons, felt markers, water colors etc.
—Pass out the paper.

Appreciation:
—Walk around to look at the work—encourage, offer help if needed, etc.
—Admire their finished product (sometimes hold it up, or let the child walk around and show it).

Folder:
   If possible have the children keep a Gospel folder for their pictures, plays, etc. Let them take the pictures home to show, if they wish, but encourage their return, as they will be useful during the Reflection.

ALTERNATIVES:

—Group work—give out large paper (brown roll paper, primary drawing paper, or smaller pieces taped together) and let groups of children work on different scenes.
—Make a banner (cloth or paper) for classroom or Eucharistic Celebration, or small ones for their rooms at home.
—Make puppet characters that can be used with play script. Some might work on scenery for the puppet play.
—Opaque projector work, reproducing Gospel scene with felt markers.
—Cut out stand-up figures in a 3-D scene.
—Symbol art, etc.
—Offer a ditto copy of a picture for those who wish to color it or use it as a model in drawing their own picture.

UNIT 19—JESUS AND THE CHILDREN

Section C—The Play

Characters: Narrator 2, a Mother, Disciples 1, 2, 3, Jesus, Narrator 1

Narrator 1:   The title of our play is:
JESUS AND THE CHILDREN
(Introduction of characters)

Narrator 2:   Then Jesus . . . went to the region of Judea and crossed the Jordan River. Again crowds came flocking to him and he taught them, as he always did.
(Mark 10, 1)

Narrator 1:   When he was finished speaking to them, the disciples and Jesus went into the house. The disciples had questions they wanted to ask. Then some people came bringing their children to Jesus.

A mother: Please ask the teacher to lay his hands on our children and bless them. Look how anxious they are to greet him.

Disciple 1:   Go away from the Master. Can't you see he is weary?

Disciple 2:   He has been teaching the crowd all day long.

Disciple 3:   The children are making too much noise. Get them away! Come back later!

Narrator 2:   When Jesus noticed it, he was angry.   (Mark 10, 14)

Jesus: Let the children come to me! Do not stop them, because the Kingdom of God belongs to such as these. Remember this! Whoever does not receive the Kingdom of God like a child will never enter it.   (Mark 10, 14-15)

Narrator 1:   Then he took the children in his arms, placed his hands on each of them and blessed them.

UNIT 19—JESUS AND THE CHILDREN

Section D—REFLECTION

Questions:

Little children loved to come to Jesus. He liked to tell grown-ups that these little ones were a good example of the Kingdom.

1. Why did the disciples want to keep the children away from Jesus?

2. When Jesus noticed the children going off, what did he say?

3. As the children gathered around Jesus, what happened?

4. What did Jesus mean when he talked about welcoming the Kingdom as a little child?

5. Is the Kingdom of God easy enough for every person in the world to understand?

6. What is this simple message of the Kingdom?

7. When does Jesus "touch" our lives with his message?

Prayer:

Close your eyes while we talk to Jesus. He is here with us. He listens to our prayer. We want him to TOUCH our lives. Repeat after me. (9)

> LORD JESUS,
> YOU BLESSED THE LITTLE CHILDREN.
> YOU LAID YOUR HANDS ON THEM
> AND TOUCHED THEIR LIVES.
> BLESS ME, LORD JESUS.
> LET ME LIVE THE KINGDOM.
> LET ME SPREAD YOUR MESSAGE OF LOVE.
> STAY IN TOUCH WITH MY LIFE.
> THANK YOU, LORD.
> AMEN.

UNIT 20

ZACCHAEUS

UNIT 20—ZACCHAEUS

Section A—Telling the Story

Introduction: Most publicans, or tax collectors, were not liked by the people. Some thought that they collected more money than they should and then kept some for themselves. This is why some people called them sinners. Here is the story told by St. Luke.

Repeat after me.

Jesus went . . . into *Jericho and was passing through. (*S)
There was a **chief tax collector there**, (2)
named Zacchaeus, (2)
who was **rich**. (16)

He was trying to **see** who Jesus was, (21)
but he was a **little man** and could not see . . . (28)
because of the **crowd**. (7)

So he **ran** ahead of the crowd (26)
and **climbed** a sycamore tree to **see** Jesus (6, 21)
who would be **going that way**. (19)

When **Jesus** came to that place he **looked** up (10, 21)
and **said** to Zacchaeus, (23)
"**Hurry down, Zacchaeus**, (6)
for I must **stay** in your house today." (15)

Zacchaeus **hurried down** (27)
and **welcomed him** with great joy. (7)

All the people who saw it started grumbling,
"This man has gone as a guest to the house of a sinner!" } (28)

Zacchaeus **stood up** and said to the Lord, (19)
"**Listen**, sir! (23)
I will **give** half my belongings to the poor; (16)
and if I have cheated anyone,
I will pay him back four times as much." (30)

Jesus said to him, (10)
"**Salvation** has come to this house today; (8)
this man, also, is a **descendant** of Abraham. (6)
For the **Son of Man** came to **seek and to save** the lost." (10, 17)

Luke 19, 1-10

114

UNIT 20—ZACCHAEUS

Section B—Art Form

PROCEDURE:
Set the Scene:
—Encourage a creative picture or series of pictures.
—Review the setting. Recall the different scenes of the story by asking what people were there, what the scene looked like, expressions, moods, etc.
—Show a picture from a children's Bible, or
—Put the scene on an overhead transparency or chalk the scene on the board.
Create the Mood:
—As the materials are being passed out have slow, instrumental music playing in the background. (If music was used for "Telling the Story" use the same composition during the art.)
 At the same time it might be helpful to have one or two children reread the Gospel text.
—Remind them to share their ideas with others.
Materials:
—Ask the children to take out whatever materials are needed—crayons, felt markers, water colors etc.
—Pass out the paper.
Appreciation:
—Walk around to look at the work—encourage, offer help if needed, etc.
—Admire their finished product (sometimes hold it up, or let the child walk around and show it).
Folder:
 If possible have the children keep a Gospel folder for their pictures, plays, etc. Let them take the pictures home to show, if they wish, but encourage their return, as they will be useful during the Reflection.

ALTERNATIVES:
—Group work—give out large paper (brown roll paper, primary drawing paper, or smaller pieces taped together) and let groups of children work on different scenes.
—Make a banner (cloth or paper) for classroom or Eucharistic Celebration, or small ones for their rooms at home.
—Make puppet characters that can be used with play script. Some might work on scenery for the puppet play.
—Opaque projector work, reproducing Gospel scene with felt markers.
—Cut out stand-up figures in a 3-D scene.
—Symbol art, etc.
—Offer a ditto copy of a picture for those who wish to color it or use it as a model in drawing their own picture.

UNIT 20—ZACCHAEUS

Section C—The Play

Characters: Narrator 2, Zacchaeus, Jesus, Person 1, 2, Narrator 1

Narrator 1:   The title of our play is:
ZACCHAEUS
(Introduction of characters)

Narrator 2:   Jesus was passing through Jericho. Now there was a large crowd out to see him—some were just curious to have a look at this man whom people talked about.

Narrator 1:   There was a chief tax collector there, named Zacchaeus, who was rich. He was trying to see who Jesus was, but he was a little man and could not see . . . because of the crowd. So he ran ahead . . . and climbed a sycamore tree.
(Luke 19, 2-4)

Zacchaeus: That's better. Now I'll be able to see this Jesus when he comes this way. Everyone speaks of him these days.

   (Jesus reaches the spot where Zacchaeus is and looks up.)
Jesus: Hurry down, Zacchaeus, for I must stay in your house today.   (Luke 19, 5)

Zacchaeus: What, Master! In my house! I'm coming right down.

Person 1:   What is happening? Doesn't the Master know who this publican is? Doesn't he realize that this man is a sinner, always taking our money away from us and keeping it for himself?

   (As Jesus enters the house)
Person 2:   This man has gone as a guest to the home of a sinner!   (Luke 19, 7)

   (Jesus goes into the house as the people continue to murmur outside.)
Zacchaeus: Listen, sir! I will give half my belongings to the poor; and if I have cheated anyone, I will pay him back four times as much.   (Luke 19, 8)

Jesus: Salvation has come to this house today; this man, also, is a descendant of Abraham. For the Son of Man came to seek and to save the lost.
(Luke 19, 9-10)

UNIT 20—ZACCHAEUS

Section D—REFLECTION

Questions:

Zacchaeus must have had a hard life until Jesus came along. He may have been poor afterward but he was rich in God's love.

1. Why didn't the people of Jericho like Zacchaeus?
2. What sort of a man did Jesus see in that tree? What happened?
3. Why were the people unhappy when Jesus went to the house of the man they called a sinner?
4. If they knew anything about Jesus, would they have been happy that Jesus went to that house? Why?
5. All Zacchaeus wanted to do was "see" Jesus, and just from a distance. What happened to him after Jesus got in touch with him?
6. How did Zacchaeus tell Jesus he was sorry for the past?
7. Zacchaeus was making up for his sins in a practical way. How can we make up for having hurt others?
8. How do you feel after you say you are sorry? Is it ever easy?
9. How do you feel after you have forgiven someone? Is that easy?

Prayer:

Close your eyes while we talk to Jesus. He is here with us. He listens to our prayer. He tells us to MAKE UP and be happy. Repeat after me. (16)

> LORD JESUS,
> YOU FOUND ZACCHAEUS
> AND MADE HIM A HAPPY MAN!
> I WANT TO MAKE OTHERS HAPPY.
> SHOW ME THE WAY.
> IF I HURT ANYONE,
> HELP ME TO SAY "I'M SORRY."
> THANK YOU, LORD.
> AMEN.